The Art of Angels

The Dream of St. Jerome *by Nicoli di Pietro (1394-1430). Jerome, a learned doctor of the Church of the 4th century, perhaps best known in art for presentations of him as a desert hermit suffering temptation, had a dream in which he was brought before Christ. In the dream he was whipped by angels for loving the Classics and the Latin tongue more than the Hebrew spoken by the Old Testament prophets. This led him to learn Hebrew and to his making a translation of the Bible from its Greek and Hebrew sources.* Musée du Louvre, Paris.

PAGE 1
Detail from The Last Judgement *by Fra Angelico (c. 1387-1455). Angels here perform a circle dance with saved souls in Paradise. Fra Angelico originally worked as a miniaturist and the decorated ground and complexity of the content have more in common with his manuscript work than with his simpler frescoes.* Museo di San Marco dell'Angelico, Florence.

The Art of *Angels*

Regency House
Publishing Ltd.

Howard Loxton

Angel Musicians *by Giovanni Martini*
(*d. 1535*). Museo Civico, Udine.

**Published in 1995 by Regency House
Publishing Limited**
The Grange
Grange Yard
London
SE1 3AG

ISBN 1 85361 413 0

Printed & bound by ORIENTAL PRESS, (DUBAI).

Contents

Introduction

What do you have in your mind when you think of an angel? Most people will imagine a person, probably someone rather beautiful, wearing a long, loosely pleated garment reaching to the feet and belted at the waist: but unlike a human this being has wings. The wings are not like those of a bird, replacing the arms, but something extra, very large and arching upwards. If you imagine an angel from the front, you do not see where his or her wings grow from and even from the back you cannot see how they are attached for they seem to emerge directly through the garment without disturbing it. Your idea of an angel has been formed by the many similar images which artists have created over the past centuries when representing angels in religious paintings and sculptures. But that is only one way of visualizing angels. Angels can take many forms.

The concept of an angel has not been a static one and it can be found in cultures other than those embraced by the monotheistic religions in which angels especially feature. Although Judaism, Christianity and Islam all include angels in their cosmology, the information given about them in the sacred texts of the three religions – the Old and New Testaments of the Holy Bible and the Holy Qur'an – gives no definitive explanation of angels and their role but presumes some existing understanding among the faithful which does not require reiteration. In later times, rabbis, imams and priests have developed their own theories about angels and their roles. Some of their concerns and ideas now seem to have little relevance to the message of religion or the lives of the faithful today and some people would discount angels altogether or prefer to see them as a symbol rather than a reality. Nevertheless, they are an essential element of Islam, play an important part in the history of Israel, as recounted in the Bible, and they are still part of the tenets of belief which Christians, both Roman Catholic and Protestant, subscribe to when they repeat the Creed. Martin Luther abandoned the concept of an angel hierarchy but he held firmly to a belief in Satan and his hordes, whom traditional belief envisage as fallen angels.

This book is not written by a theologian. It describes some of the ideas which people have had about angels but does not seek to endorse any particular viewpoint. It sets out to present the wide variety of ways in which people have thought of angels and attempted to depict them, to explain some of the background to that iconography and the incidents and concepts which have inspired particular pictures.

Jewish, Christian and Islamic doctrines all forbid the worship of idols and in both Judaism and Islam this has at times been interpreted as a ban on figurative art, though at other periods or where the religious teachers differed in their interpretation, this has been permitted in private, as fine work by both Jewish and Moslem artists shows. In Persian, Moghul and Turkish art especially, representational art has been highly developed and has even included depictions of the Prophet and of angels; however, most of the illustrations that follow are drawn from Christian religious art and occasionally from secular sources. To prevent the possibility of treating images as idols much Islamic art has deliberately tended to be two-dimensional or otherwise made clear that it is symbolic rather than representational, though religious bans on image making do not seem, even in the most fundamentalist Islamic states, to prevent the use of photography, film and television, especially where political leaders are concerned. However, it is only those who have studied Islam deeply who can make such careful distinctions. Sectarian differences among Christians, as well as in the other faiths, make certain concepts acceptable or not. The paintings and other artworks in this book are presented as a record of the way in which painters and sculptors have responded to the subject.

The reader will find considerable variation in both image and theory, which are at times bound to conflict with strongly held beliefs; but this will enlarge his or her understanding of the many ways in which a religious idea can be interpreted and provide some magnificent examples drawn from the art of many centuries.

Biblical quotations throughout are given in the English translation of King James' Authorised Version of the Holy Bible.

LEFT
The Virgin in a Rose Arbour *by Stephan Lochner (fl. 1442-d. 1451). Juvenile angels who seem hardly older than the Christ child offer music, fruit and worship while above two angels pull back a hanging to reveal God in heaven surrounded by angel faces. Two of the angels have wings bearing a peacock feather pattern which recalls descriptions, in various books of revelation, of angels being covered with eyes, while the blue outer feathers of the others may indicate that they are cherubim.* Wallraf-Richartz Museum, Cologne.

What are Angels?

The English word angel, and similar words in European languages, come from the Greek *angelos*, through the Latin *angelus*. The Greek meaning is a messenger or courier, as is that of the Persian *angaros*. The earlier Sanskrit *angiras* was used to describe a divine spirit but the ancient Greeks used *angelos,* first for ordinary human messengers and then too, for messengers from the gods. These might take any form from Hermes, the message carrier of the Olympians, to birds and other means of communication employed by the gods. The angel as a specific type of being is not an ancient Greek concept but it does go back to the very beginnings of the Jewish Old Testament tradition in the Hebrew *mal'akh* (which in Arabic became the *mala'ika* of Islam), and along with so much other Jewish lore was carried through into Christian belief. A declaration by the Council of Nicaea in 325 B.C. declared a belief in angels a part of the official dogma of the Christian Church.

Jewish angels were seen specifically as messengers of God, though this was only one of their functions. *Genesis*, the first book of the Old Testament, which describes the creation of heaven and earth, does not say when angels came into being: but on expelling Adam and Eve from the Garden of Eden, God places cherubim to the east to guard it.

The creatures of earth are made from earth but angels must have been part of heaven. In Islamic belief, angels are spirits created from air, while Judaic tradition suggests that 'the essence of the angels is fire, they sustain themselves in fire and their fiery breath consumes man'. They are usually conceived of as spiritual rather than physical beings, but appear or are envisaged in many forms. However, there have been those who have believed that angels have material form, among them such Christian theologians as the 3rd-century Origen of Alexandria, the 11th-century Cistercian St. Bernard of Clairvaux, and the 13th-century Franciscan St. Bonaventure.

Some Jewish theologians allotted the making of the angels to the second day of Creation and others to the fifth, while the *Book of Enoch* has angels present even before the Creation.

Enoch is the name of two biblical characters: the eldest son of Cain and 'the seventh from Adam', the father of Methuselah. This may not be a literal seventh for the number seven, which features so often as a magical number, was used as a symbol of perfection and may indicate that he was a perfect man. He was described in *Genesis* as walking with God and, when he was 969 years old 'he was not: for God took him'. This is usually taken to mean that he did not die but was taken up into heaven, like the later prophet Elijah (see pages 33 and 48). Some non-canonical sources equate him with the angel Metatron and with Elijah he becomes one of the 'two witnesses' of the End of the World mentioned in the *Book of Revelation*.

The *Book of Enoch*, which describes a vision in which Enoch is shown all the regions of earth, heaven and hell, is one of the most important sources of angel lore. It is thought to have been written in the 2nd century B.C., either as a new text or based on earlier versions. The oldest known text was found in Ethiopia. There are other books also attributed to him and they were all accepted as part of scripture by early Christians. Like the books of the *Apocrypha*, they were rejected by St. Jerome in the 4th century A.D. but they had already had an important influence on angelology.

The *Apocrypha* are books thought to have been for the most part written during the Jewish exile in Babylon and up to the first century A.D. They were included in the Greek version of the Old Testament but not translated into Hebrew, and include the *Book of Tobit*, which gives one of the most detailed the angel stories (see pages 50-51). Protestants accept these books as suitable for moral instruction but not for doctrinal purposes, though in the 16th century the Council of Trent decided that they carried the same authority as other books of the Bible, and the Eastern Churches follow the same line.

The Ramparts of God's House *by John Melhuish Strudwick (1849-1937). With the exception of the recording angel, all the main angels here appear to be female and, although the blank eyes of all except the angel with roses and a pair of inquisitive angels looking* through the window help to counter the sensuality created by the concentration on the naked souls, there is still a hint of the titillation found in 'classical' subjects of this period. Christie's, London.

Talmudic writings develop the concept of angels and the Kabbalists, followers of a mystical Judaic tradition, identified and named many more individual angels, often finding inspiration for these new creations in pagan sources. Further Christian ideas on angels were developed by Dionysius the Areopagite, a 5th- or 6th-century Platonist, and argument on the nature of angels and the hierarchies of heaven continued to exercise churchmen and occultists for centuries. This reached an amazing level, so much so that during the Middle Ages there was serious and heated debate as to exactly how many angels could be accommodated on the head of a pin!

The theories of the theologians have been endorsed and modified by poets and painters and it is perhaps more from art and literature than from the doctors of divinity that the universal idea of angels has been created. In works such as Dante Alighieri's *La Divina Commedia* and John Milton's *Paradise Lost,* concepts drawn from others have been reinforced and, because of their acknowledged literary importance and foundation in the Christian religion, their presentation of angels and of heaven and earth have been absorbed into the mainstream of Western culture. These books were written as poetic allegories rather than accounts of divine inspiration which the *Book of Revelation* or the *Book of Enoch* claim to be: but their imagery is clear, and they do not need the same complex decoding as the visionary texts.

Even more accessible are the painted and sculpted images of angels. Over the centuries, the way in which they have been represented has changed. When works of art were mostly commissioned for sacred or devotional purposes, the artist would have been expected to conform to current ecclesiastical beliefs as well as artistic conventions. Although, in later years, angels often appear in secular surroundings the general acceptance of what they might look like had by then been firmly established.

There is not just one kind of angel in the Heavenly Host. Most people will have heard of cherubim, seraphim, archangels and angels, all of whom find mention in the Bible: but in the Old Testament you will also find the Hebrew ophanim (wheels or chariots) and St. Paul in his epistles speaks of powers, virtues, principalities, dominions and thrones.

Madonna under a Baldachino *by Sandro Botticelli (1440-1510). Botticelli's angels are very like the winds and nymphs in his* Birth of Venus *and have considerable animation.* Biblioteca Ambrosiana, Milan.

Very few angels are given individual names in Scripture, though non-canonical texts have provided many others, sometimes assimilating pagan deities and heroes into the angel host and providing names for angels thought to have particular responsibilities. There are thought to be many millions of angels; Kabbalists in the 14th century calculated a precise figure of 301,655,722, so a complete census would be very difficult to make, especially if all the stars in heaven are counted as angels, as the writer of the *Book of Revelation* believed they should be. An extensive roll call was provided by the late Gustav Davidson in his *A Dictionary of Angels*, an intriguing work of reference indispensable to angelologists, first published in 1967 and still in print. There are very few names in use that he missed in his researches.

The Bible makes frequent reference to one angel, not given a personal name, but identified as the Angel of the Lord. There are other angels who bring messages direct from God but this angel has sometimes been interpreted as the form which God himself takes when wishing to make direct contact with the human race. The Bible texts have been copied or translated many times before arriving at their present versions: in the same way different versions have translated the same word sometimes as messenger and sometimes as angel making it uncertain whether the carrier is human or angelic. Sometimes this occurs in contexts where God himself has already spoken and it is thought that earlier copyists may have considered the direct naming of God as improper and used the phrase 'Angel of the Lord' as a more respectful way of referring to Him.

What do the different types of angels look like? There are paintings and illuminated manuscripts in which the artists have depicted wheels and thrones exactly as the names suggest. The first chapter of the visionary *Book of Ezekiel* is one of the sources to which these artists were trying to give expression. Its first chapter (see panel) appears to be describing cherubim and ophanim. Several chapters later, Ezekiel again sees the sapphire throne and God apparently riding on a cherub, while below the throne are cherubim and four wheels with fire between them, which he describes again in a similar manner. In the *Talmud*, the cherubim are equated with the ophanim, so perhaps this should be

interpreted as a composite angel form.

The prophet Isaiah had a vision of the seraphim surrounding the heavenly throne. As he describes them 'each one had six wings; with twain he covered his face, and with twain he covered his feet, and with twain he did fly.' The *Book of Enoch* confirms Isaiah's description of the seraphim.

Ezekiel speaks of a man clad in white linen who seems to be a form of angel and since the human shape is the one in which angels most often appear as messengers to men (though angels, if non-corporeal could presumably take any form), this is the one which is most often seen in Renaissance and later painting, while cherubim are differentiated as chubby infants, often with only their heads and wings in evidence.

Where do these images of angels come from? Whatever the nature of spiritual belief, their interpretation in physical form is likely to be influenced by existing ideas and images. Christianity and Islam being monotheistic religions, can envisage only one God. But although the God of Israel demanded the Jews worship only Him, they were surrounded by deities and images of other religions who were bound to acquire a spurious credibility from the fact that their own God was so obviously in conflict with them. It was also inevitable that they absorbed much from the cultures with which they were in contact. During the 5th and 6th centuries B.C., during their exile in Babylon, the Jews were especially influenced by Chaldean ideology – and it should not be forgotten that Abraham himself came from the Chaldean city of Ur. Zoroastrianism has its own hierarchy of celestial spirits, both good and bad, and in later centuries Greek influence may also have been present. Certainly, in the period when Christian iconography was being established, the mythological forms of the classical world were extremely influential.

The idea of the cherub, the angel form which guards the gates of Eden, has many affinities with the great winged figures which guarded the temples and palaces of Assyria. The word has its roots in the Akkadian *karibu*, meaning 'one who prays' or 'one who intercedes' bearing a direct corollary with the later concept of the angelic being. The guardians at Nineveh and Nimrud have bodies of bulls and lions with human faces, but there are other Assyrian figures too: the

'And I looked, and, behold, a whirlwind came out of the north, a great cloud, and a fire infolding itself, and a brightness was about it, and out of the midst thereof as the colour of amber, out of the midst of the fire.

Also out of the midst thereof came the likeness of four living creatures. And this was their appearance; they had the likeness of a man. And every one had four faces, and every one had four wings. And their feet were straight feet; and the sole of their feet was like the sole of a calf's foot: and they sparkled like the colour of burnished brass. And they had the hands of a man under their wings on their four sides; and they four had their faces and their wings.

Their wings were joined one to another; they turned not when they went; they went every one straight forward. As for the likeness of their faces, they four had the face of a man, and the face of a lion, on the right side: and they four had the face of an ox on the left side; they four also had the face of an eagle. Thus were their faces: and their wings were stretched upward; two wings of every one were joined one to another, and two covered their bodies. And they went every one straight forward: whither the spirit was to go, they went; and they turned not when they went.

As for the likeness of the living creatures, their appearance was like coals of fire, and like the appearance of lamps: it went up and down among the living creatures; and the fire was bright, and out of the fire went forth lightning. And the living creatures ran and returned as the appearance of a flash of lightning.

Now as I beheld the living creatures, behold one wheel upon the earth by the living creatures, with his four faces. The appearance of the wheels and their work was like unto the colour of beryl: and they four had one likeness: and their appearance and their work was as it were a wheel in the middle of a wheel. When they went, they went upon their four sides: and they turned not when they went.

As for their rings, they were so high that they were dreadful; and their rings were full of eyes round about them four...

... And above the firmament over their heads was the likeness of a throne, as the appearance of a sapphire stone: and upon the likeness of the throne was the likeness as the appearance of a man above upon it.

And I saw as the colour of amber, as the appearance of fire round about within it, from the appearance of his loins even upward, and from the appearance of his loins even downward, I saw as it were the appearance of fire, and it had brightness round about.

As the appearance of the bow that is in the cloud in the day of rain, so was the appearance of the brightness round about. This was the appearance of the likeness of the glory of the Lord. And when I saw it, I fell upon my face, and I heard a voice of one that spake.'

Book of Ezekiel *Chapter 1*

An Egyptian Tapestry of the 5th-6th century, originally part of a curtain, probably Coptic. A cross within the wreath supported by the angel identifies it as a Christian angel.
Victoria and Albert Museum, London.

اوشیطان اوشته مندی شیطان انا الوبرح جطه اللدیکو کوتشدن رنده د کارت صدر نشته مصال مرتشده درزن زن نشه شیلینه اوتویربل ملکنه قصه رعنیف
اسوعفام رح کعمانی رجماعرماراتم اولیوب رجنی طون علیدا نوح طون انی وفناعن بلزیئشی شبایات نمرالدی استو انی ودر دانی خطای استوالوجارائمی رصربلازانه کلیه شیاطرض

The prophet Enoch attended by angels in a 16th-century Turkish miniature. Topkapi Museum, Istanbul.

ugallos and genii (precursors of the Islamic jinns), who on palace walls protected kings such as Nebuchadnezzar, are human-bodied though are sometimes given an animal or eagle head. They often carry what appears to be a handbag, in fact a pail of lustral water, while in the other hand they hold a fir cone with which to sprinkle it to keep off evil spirits. They are frequently shown in palace reliefs accompanying the king, exactly like a guardian angel – and they have two pairs of wings.

In later portrayals of angels the influence of the art of the classical period is most apparent. The garments worn by angels seem to be based on the *peplos*, an item of classical Greek costume worn by women but which somehow seems to have been adopted as the garb of angels,

whether they appear in male or female form. The similarity between the various representations of angels and the figures of Eros (either as a youth or chubby Cupid) and the Erates, of Nike, the Winged Victory, of Eos, goddess of Dawn, of Boreas, the North Wind and his fellows and so many other winged creatures from classical mythology often makes it difficult to distinguish the Christian from the mythological if the context does not make it clear. The little cherubs, from which we get the expression *cherubic*, so unlike the frightening guardians which they were first, are interchangeable with the putti or amorini in a Pompeiian fresco.

Religious texts speak of angels, covered in eyes, which are sometimes shown as the eyes of peacocks' feathers

in their wings, and endowed with an extreme radiance and vividness of colour. The multi-winged cherubim and seraphim of the texts and paintings of earlier centuries seldom appear in more modern works and it is rare after the Middle Ages to see an angel depicted multi-headed.

In the centuries when Christian religious art was not only created for the Church but mainly by monks in monasteries, the artist might have some familiarity with the angelic theories of the doctors of the Church, but as painting and sculpture became secularized, ideas of how angels were supposed to look were influenced by a general assumption of conventional beauty and purity as symbolic of their holiness.

The Hierarchies of Heaven

According to angel lore, heaven is not an egalitarian society. Not only is God, as one would expect, omnipotently and unquestionably the King of Kings, there is a hierarchical and, one suspects, a highly bureaucratic system that is much like that of the modern world. Opinions as to the exact organization of that hierarchy differ. St. Paul, in his epistles to the Ephesians, Romans and Corinthians, names powers, authorities, principalities, dominations and thrones, but he does not place them in relation to each other or to the seraphim, cherubim, ophanim, archangels and any undifferentiated angels. Indeed, can one be sure that these are all individual varieties of angel and not alternative ways of referring to the very same type?

If they are all different types, then this provides ten different ranks of angel; but schemes worked out by the main angelologists have varied from St. Jerome's seven to the twelve listed by Francis Barret in *The Magus* at the beginning of the 19th century (they included innocents, martyrs and confessors). Several of the kabbalistic schemes, using Hebrew names, have ten.

In general, the Christian hierarchies place seraphim and cherubim at the top and archangels and angels at the bottom. This is the order followed by Dionysius the Areopagite and Thomas Aquinas, and used by Dante in *La Divina Commedia* (except that he places principalities between archangels and angels):

1 Seraphim
2 Cherubim
3 Thrones
4 Dominations
5 Virtues
6 Powers
7 Principalities
8 Archangels
9 Angels

Virtues, which are comparable to the *mal'akhim* or the *tarshishim* of Hebrew lore, are confusingly considered to include several named angels who are

The Assumption of the Virgin, *altarpiece for the burial chapel of Matteo Palmieri, attributed to Francesco di Giovanni, called Botticini (c.1446-1497). Below, on either side of the Virgin's flower-filled coffin and in front of a view of Florence and Fiesole with a farm owned by him, kneels the deceased, a civil servant, faced by his widow dressed as a Benedictine nun, landscape from the Val d'Elsa which formed part of her dowry behind her. Above them the nine choirs of heaven welcome the virgin. Highest are the Councillors: seraphim, cherabim and thrones; then the Governors: dominations, virtues and powers; next Ministers: principalities, archangels and angels. Saints and prophets are shown seated among the tiers of angels. Palmieri heretically believed humans to be descended from angels that did not take sides when Satan rebelled. Here they regain their places.* National Gallery, London.

15

also archangels. Among ranks in other schemes are hosts, perhaps the warriors, (though the term is more frequently used to signify all angels), and aeons, which gnostics considered the first created beings.

Different concepts of creation have visualized the universe with heaven, earth and hell divided into different worlds or 'mansions', the number of each frequently being the mystical number seven. The *Book of Enoch* (which if really by him would date from before the Flood!) describes a journey through the heavens which at times reads as though he is describing a terrestrial trip in the Middle East of his own time. In his record, hell is actually placed within the third heaven. The Jewish concept is of seven heavens linked to seven earths, but Christian thinking places hell beneath the earth and develops the concept of hell as a place of eternal punishment. Purgatory is seen as a half-way house for those in need of further purification before entering heaven: limbo is the place where those free of sin who have died unbaptized, or before Christ came to save the world, await the final resurrection.

Dante offers a tour of all these worlds in *La Divina Commedia*. Hell is suspended below the earth as a pit surrounded by ledges on which sinners are grouped according to the nature of their sins. He envisages heaven as part of the Ptolemaic system with the earth as centre of the universe surrounded by encircling spheres. Motionless at their centre is the bright star of the Godhead, too dazzling for the naked eye to behold, set in the Empyrean outside time and space, which communicates its 'virtue' or power to the ninth or Crystalline Heaven. This is the Primum Mobile which is the sphere of the seraphim from which it is passed to the eighth heaven, that of the cherubim and the fixed stars and so downwards. As Dante (in Henry Cary's English translation) has Beatrice explain:

'In the first circles, they, whom thou beheld'st,
Are Seraphim and Cherubim. Thus swift
Follow their hoops, in likeness to the point,
Near as they can aproaching; and they can
The more the loftier their vision. Those
That round them fleet, gazing the Godhead next,
Are Thrones; in whom the first trine ends.
      and all
Are blessed, even as their sight descends
Deeper into the Truth, wherein rest is
For every mind. Thus happiness hath root

Illustration by Gustave Doré (1833-1883) for Dante's La Divina Commedia. *Circles of heavenly choirs surround Dante and Beatrice in Paradise.*

In seeing, not in loving, which of sight
Is aftergrowth. And of the seeing such
The need, as unto each, in due degree,
Grace and good will their measure have assigned.

The other trine, that still with opening buds
In this eternal springtide blossom fair,
Fearless of bruising from the nightly ram,
Breathe up in warbled melodies threefold
Hosannas, blending ever; from the three,
Transmitted, hierarchy of gods, for aye
Rejoicing; Dominations first; next them,
Virtues; and Powers the third; the next to whom
Are Princedoms and Archangels, with glad round
To tread their festal ring; and last, the band
Angelical, disporting in their sphere.'

מקדש

זה הכרובים פורשים כנפים מעל הכפרת ושולחן הזהב

An illumination from a 13th-century Hebrew manuscript showing six-winged cherubim over the Ark of the Covenant. God instructed Moses in fashioning the ark to 'make two cherubim of gold, of beaten work shalt thou make them, in the two ends of the mercy seat. And the cherubims shall stretch forth their wings on high, covering the mercy seat with their wings, and their faces shall look one to another.'

It would appear that the angels have great powers as they ascend to the higher heavens, each order controlling one of the heavens and its influence. The seraphim are the closest to God, burning with the fire of Love and according to Jewish doctrine ceaselessly chanting the Hebrew 'Kadosh, Kadosh, Kadosh' (Holy, Holy, Holy). According to Enoch there were only four seraphim, corresponding to the four main directions or the four winds, but later this was interpreted to mean that there were four chief seraphs, in command of the others.

The cherubim are imbued with knowledge, though as has already been mentioned they have a role as protectors and guardian spirits; they also give unceasing praise to the Creator. Rabbinical writings see them as personifications of the winds and bearers of His throne or His charioteers.

The thrones (or wheels or ophanim) of the seventh heaven are thought of as the actual chariots. The dominions or dominations of the sixth heaven are said by Enoch to regulate angels' duties.

The virtues of the fifth heaven are associated with those heroes who struggle for good; they bestow virtue and blessing, usually by assisting at the performance of miracles.

The powers of the fourth heaven have as their main duty the keeping of order on the 'heavenly pathways'. Dionysius placed them between the first and second heavens and Enoch saw their task as preventing demons from overthrowing the world. They are said to be in charge of human souls and to help keep each individual soul in balance.

The principalities of the third heaven are protectors of religion; they watch over leaders and rulers and appear to be responsible for particular countries, cities or peoples.

The second heaven is that of the archangels, though archangels also seem to have leading roles in charge of other heavens. Dionysius considered them the messengers 'which carry Divine Decrees' and they are the angels which are given individual names in both the Bible and the Qur'an (see pages 22-33).

The first and lowest heaven is that of the angels who carry no other appellation. Enoch (whose schema has only seven heavens – hence the expression 'being in seventh heaven' as being in a state of bliss) places the angels in charge of the stars and weather.

Jewish and Christian theorists and mystics have suggested many different concepts of heaven and Islam offers its own interpretation. The great religions promise a place where there is perfect happiness, where earthly desires no longer exist. But all descriptions of heaven are allegorical. The garden heaven of Islam with its myriad delights is a dream of perfection, divested of all carnality and offering joy and happiness without base desire.

If our image of heaven is so uncertain, it is just as difficult to conceive of angels and their role within it, particularly when the matter of the fallen angels (pages 34-37) remains to be considered. The roles of the 'good' angels are easier to imagine.

As messengers and intermediaries, the angels bring news and revelations from God and carry prayers and information back to heaven. The idea of a ladder between heaven and earth, as in Jacob's dream, was a necessary concept before angels were envisaged as being able to fly to heaven. Now the tenets of religion, rituals given to the Jews by God, demonstrated by Christ and revealed to the Prophet Muhammad by observing the angels' praise of God, are the continuing ladder of communication between heaven and earth.

The protecting spirit is common to many religions, often linked to places as well as people. Angels may have responsibilities for inanimate objects but guardian angels are associated with people or groups of people, both as guide and protector. It has been suggested that we may each also have a complementary 'evil' angel to tempt us to chose the path of evil. Even if the guardian angel operates alone, there is a theory that if its influence is continually ignored it will gradually withdraw its protection.

Angels can be agents of punishment or chastisement, God's champions and defenders of the faithful. The word 'seraphim' may have etymological links with the word 'serpent' in old Middle-Eastern languages and the fiery serpents sent to bite those who opposed Moses (*Numbers 21: 6*) are thought by some to have been seraphim. Although the dragon has more often been used as a symbol of evil forces in the Judaeo-Christian-Islamic tradition, the serpent has a positive role in many others as a symbol of life and healing. Could there be a connection there with the seraphim as healers? Certainly angels could be the agents of cures and miracles.

Angels have generally been considered sexless: the Jews symbolized this fact by standing them with their feet together. But the association of virtues with the feminine has led to them being embued with an overall effeminate quality, both in dress and facial appearance in many depictions of them. Alternatively they may be given an idealized male beauty. The story of the fall (see page 34) implies that they may have possessed a latent sexuality, capable of being aroused by humans, after they had been created, if not by their own

A six-winged seraph standing on one of the ophanim, from Christian Iconography *by Adolphe Napoléon Didron, 1886.*

kind. Certainly some of the cherubim painted by baroque artists as little putti have male organs and in more recent times Jacob Epstein caused some scandal when he carved a figure of Lucifer that was gloriously male.

Even while performing earthly duties, angels are considered capable of turning their faces to God in heaven, unless descriptions of this kind are allegories meaning that their work on earth is itself a form of praise.

That praise is generally conceived of as musical, for if the turning of the heavenly spheres creates music, as the ancients believed it did, how much more glorious must be the sound that is offered to God. Indeed, the orders of the angels are usually known as choirs. Scripture suggests that angel musicians can descend from the heavens, as did the heavenly host when they joined the shepherds' announcing angel at the time of Christ's Nativity: angel musicians frequently appear in pictures of the Nativity itself and in paintings where saints are welcomed into heaven.

Ophanim (wheels, or thrones) in an interpretation of this order of angels from Christian Iconography *by Adolphe Napoléon Didron, 1886.*

'Though they are so great, so glorious, so pure, so wonderful, that the very sight of them (if we were allowed to see them) would strike us to the earth, as it did the prophet Daniel, holy and righteous as he was, yet they are our fellow-servants and our fellow-workers, and they carefully watch over and defend the humblest of us.'

Cardinal Newman

The Virgin Enthroned, *from the Vallombrosa altarpiece by Pietro (Vanucci) Perugino (c. 1445-1523). The Virgin Mary is encircled by a choir of cherubim, their chubby faces protruding from multiple wings, while other angels support her throne, play for her, and attend on God above.* Galleria dell'Accademia, Florence.

The Archangels

The archangels are only the second order in the generally accepted hierarchy of angels but St. Paul refers to Michael as an archangel and Michael, according to the *Book of Daniel*, is 'one of the chief princes' and the one responsible for the nation of Israel which makes him at least of the higher order of principalities. Other named archangels are also assigned to rule in higher orders: Gabriel among the seraphim, Raphael among the ophanim, while all these three are sometimes named as the ruling princes of the virtues. The seven angels which the *Book of Revelation* describes standing before God are also usually interpreted as archangels.

Enoch names seven archangels: Uriel, who rules the world and Tartarus; Raguel, who takes vengeance on the world of the luminaries; Michael, who is set over the most part of mankind and over chaos; Saraquael, who is set over the spirits; Gabriel, ruler of paradise, the serpents and the cherubim; Ramiel, whom God set over those who rise; and Raphael, who rules the spirits of men. He places only four around God's throne, backed up by their followers: Michael, Raphael, Gabriel and one named Phanuel (probably synonymous with Ramiel) who is responsible for overseeing the repentance of sinners. Where lists of seven are given the most frequent other names are Uriel, Metatron, Sariel (which could be a variant of Saraquael), Anael and Raziel.

Later lists of archangels vary the names, many probably being alternative names for the same angels, and one post-Talmudic source increases the number to twelve, linking them with the signs of the zodiac, while kabbalists name nine, with Metatron named first and then repeated as a tenth.

The Qur'an mentions four archangels, naming only Jibra'il (Gabriel) and Mika'il (Michael) – the other two being Azrael, another form of Raphael, Angel of Death, and Israfel, Angel of Music who plays the flute at the end of the day and will sound the trumpet that wakes the dead on the Day of Judgement. These angels were not created at the same time. Israfel was first, Mika'il was created 5000 years later, Jibra'il after another 500 years and and perhaps Azrael later still.

Attempts have often been made to link biblical references to angelic visitations of particular archangels but authorities often disagree: Michael, Uriel, Gabriel and Ramiel have all been credited with defeating the 185,000-strong Assyrian army of Sennacherib in 701 B.C.

The syllable 'el' or 'il' at the end of angel and of so many angel names means 'bright', 'shining' or 'shining being'. It appears in several languages and can be found in Anglo-Saxon names such as Aelfrid and the English folk spirit 'elf'.

The Archangel Michael

The Archangel Michael, whose name means 'who is as God', is generally considered to be the foremost of the seven archangels and the leader of the Host of Heaven. He is the prince who defended the Israelites and later, it was claimed, the Christian Church, when as guardian he may be called on (sometimes with Gabriel) to defend church doors against the devil. According to the *Book of Revelations*, 'Michael and his angels' are described fighting 'the dragon and his angels' with the result that 'that old serpent, called the Devil, and Satan ... he was cast out into the earth, and his angels were cast out with him'. Hence Michael is often shown fighting or overcoming a dragon armed with spear or sword as God's warrior. The second-century *Testament of Abraham* presents him as so close to God that his intercession can even rescue souls from Hell and he is sometimes shown leading souls to heaven. The Roman Liturgy for the Dead used to include the antiphon 'May Michael the standard-bearer lead them into the holy light, which you promised of old to Abraham and his seed.'

Like the Egyptian god Anubis, who supervised the rites of passage to the underworld, Michael is responsible for

St. Michael, *by Bernardino Zenale (1436-1526). A wary and rather unwarlike archangel, shown in both his warrior role as devil slayer and as weigher of souls. The rather anthropomorphic dragon, still with two pairs of rudimentary wings, is a reminder that this was also once a high angel.*

St. Michael and the Dragon *by Bartoloméo Bermejo (fl. 1474-1498). The archangel, in glittering golden armour, strikes at the grotesque devil. His red wings and cloak lining indicate that he is a member of the seraphim. The donor of the painting is shown on a smaller scale, kneeling in supplication and with a sword perhaps to indicate that he too wishes to be a warrior for Christ.*

weighing souls in the balance, good deeds set against the bad. Hermes, the classical conductor of souls, was identified with Anubis and the serpent twining on his caduceus also connects him to Michael and his dragon. Hilltop sites dedicated to Mercury – many associated with legendary dragons – often became the sites of chapels and churches dedicated to the Archangel who is frequently given the title of Saint.

It was Constantine who built a church in his honour at Sosthenion, near Constantinople, where it was the sick who particularly invoked his aid. An apparition of Michael on Mount Gargano in southern Italy in 530, instructing that a cave used for pagan worship should be consecrated as a church, helped to spread his cult to the west. In 590, when Romans were dying of the plague, Pope Gregory arranged a penitential procession at which Michael appeared, above the mausoleum of Hadrian, sheathing his sword to indicate that the plague was over. Known since as the Castel Sant'Angelo, a figure of Michael was later set above it and a basilica dedicated to him was built on the Salarian Way, the Feast of St. Michael on 29 September, being that of its dedication. St. Michael's Mount in Cornwall, commemorating his appearance there in the 8th century, and Mont St-Michel in Brittany across the English Channel are two other well known foundations in his name, while in Ireland he is associated with Skellig in Co. Derry. His popularity was shown by the 686 churches dedicated to him in England alone by the end of the Middle Ages.

The Persians knew Michael as Beshter 'who provides sustenance for mankind' and in Islamic tradition he brings food and riches to those who need them. The Islamic Mika'il was described with wings of green topaz and covered from head to foot with saffron hair, each hair having a million faces, which in a million different dialects implore the pardon of God for the sins of the faithful over whom they weep. It is in the 70,000 tears from each of their eyes that the cherubim have their origin.

The Archangel Gabriel

Gabriel, whose name means 'God is my strength', explained to Daniel his vision of a ram and a billy-goat foretelling Alexander the Great's conquest of Persia and a prophecy foretelling the freeing of

Saints Michael and Gabriel, *a Greek icon of c.1700 of the two archangels (Michael in armour).*
Private Collection.

the Israelites. In both these cases the archangel is mentioned by name but it has also been suggested that Gabriel is the angel who wrestles with Jacob in the form of a man and that he was involved in the destruction of Sodom and Gommorah. Enoch says that Gabriel was sent to destroy the giant children of the fallen 'watchers' (see page 34) and did so by turning them against each other. In

An illuminated page from Les Très Riches Heures du Duc de Berry. *Against a sky of clouds from which cherubim watch the contest (except for the one who supports the arms of France) the Archangel Michael fights the dragon above Mont Saint-Michel, off the coast of Normandy, where he was said to have once appeared.* Musée Condé, Chantilly.

The Archangel Michael as seen by Adam in John Milton's *Paradise Lost*:

'... I descry
From yonder blazing cloud that veils the hill,
One of the heavenly host! and, by his gait,
None of the meanest; some great Potentate
Or of the Thrones above; such majesty
Invests his coming! yet not terrible,
That I should fear; nor sociably mild,
As Raphael, that I should much confide;
But solemn and sublime; whom not to offend,
With reverence I must meet, and thou retire.
He ended: and the Archangel soon drew nigh,
Not in his shape celestial, but as man
Clad to meet man; over his lucid arms
A military vest of purple flow'd,
Livelier than Meliboean, or the grain
Of Serra, worn by kings and heroes old
In time of truce; Iris had dipp'd the woof;
His starry helm unbuckled show'd him prime
In manhood where youth ended; by his side,
As in a glistering zodiac, hung sword,
Satan's dire dread; and in his hand the spear.'

Paradise Lost, Gabriel is the chief of the angels guarding Paradise. In view of his New Testament role he may also be the angel that appears to ancient patriarchs and their barren wives who are to conceive in their old age. (See pages 40-41, 48)

In the New Testament, Gabriel is the Angel of the Annunciation, named by Luke as appearing to the Virgin Mary and by inference usually thought to be the angel who appears to Zacharias to announce the coming birth of John the Baptist and to Joseph to tell him not to reject his pregnant wife. Is it Gabriel, too, who appears to the shepherds and the wise men? With so many angels at his disposal God surely had no need to use

the same messenger (see pages 52-57).

It is Gabriel who is traditionally the angel who appears to Jesus in the Garden of Gethsemane to give him comfort during his Agony (see page 64).

The Feast of Gabriel is celebrated in the Eastern Church on 26 March, in the West it was two days earlier but has now been combined with those of Michael and Raphael on 29 September. His association with so many births made Gabriel the patron saint of childbirth and in 1926 Pope Benedict XV declared him to be patron of post-offices, telephones and telegraph and by extension is now associated with television, radio and telecommunications.

Gabriel, in his Arabic form of Jibra'il is the angel who transmits the Qur'an to the Prophet Muhammed. At first, the Prophet is concerned that his inspiration may have come from a jinn but is then convinced, as it is put in Sura 81, that 'this is the word of a most honourable Messenger, endowed with Power, with rank before the Lord of the throne'. The suras of the Holy Qur'an were revealed at various times over a long period and were not written down to Gabriel's dictation. They were sometimes received during a vision of the archangel and sometimes implanted directly into Muhammed's mind. Remembered by him, they were related to his disciples and learned by them and written down.

Jibra'il has 1600 wings and hair of saffron, each hair embued with the brightness of the moon and stars. The sun is set between his eyes where there is also written 'There is no god but God, and Muhammed is the Prophet of God.' When he appeared to reveal the Qur'an, his green wings stretched from the eastern to the western horizon and from them millions of drops fell to become angels to glorify God.

The Archangel Raphael

In Hebrew this name means 'God heals'. Raphael is not named in the canonical books of the Bible but only in the apocryphal *Book of Tobit* as the companion and guide of young Tobias (see pages 50-51) to whom he eventually reveals himself as one of the 'seven holy angels'. In the *Book of Enoch* he is the guide to Sheol, the Judaic underworld and it was he who was sent to bind the fallen 'watcher' Asael, burying him under rocks in a desert place on earth.

From his guardianship of Tobias, Raphael is regarded as the protector of travellers and pilgrims and as his name would suggest is particularly associated with healing. He is said to have eased the pain of circumcision in the aged Abraham and to have fixed the thigh that Jacob dislocated in struggling with Gabriel. He is the patron of apothecaries. His feast day was formerly 24 October, but is now shared with Michael and Gabriel on 29 September.

The Annunciation *by Fra Angelico (c.1387-1455). Museo Diocesano, Cortona.*

FAR LEFT
The Chapel of Christ in Gethsemane,
Coventry Cathedral. The figure of an angel in
ciment fondu *by Stefen Sykes seen through*
a crown of thorns designed by Basil Spence.

BELOW
The Annunciation *from The Isenheim*
Altarpiece by Mathis Grunewald (c. 1470/80-
1528).
Unterlinden Museum, Colmar.

27

LEFT
Archangel Gabriel *by Guariento di Arpo*
(3rd quarter 14th century)
Museo Bottacin e Museo Civico, Padua.

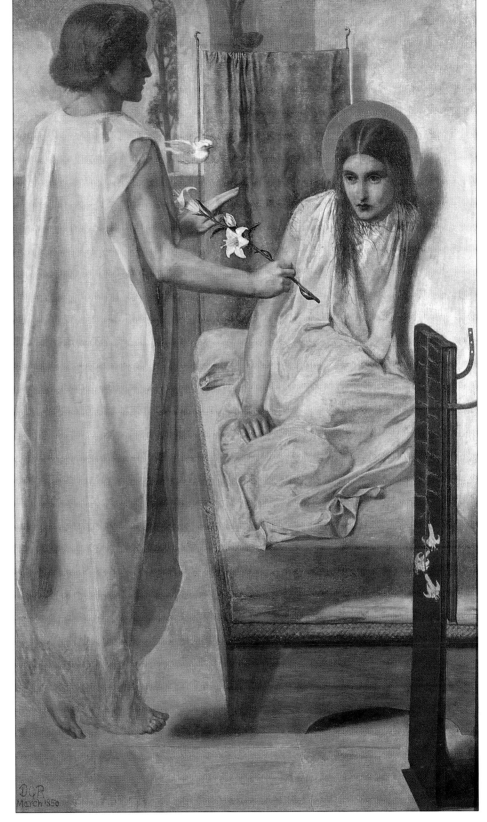

ABOVE
Angel of the Annunciation *from The Ghent*
Atarpiece by Jan van Eyck (c. 1390- 1441).
Cathedral of St. Bavo, Ghent.

RIGHT
Ecce Ancilla Domini by Dante Gabriel
Rossetti (1828-1882).
Tate Gallery, London.

Raphael when sent to the Garden of Eden:

'At once on the eastern cliff of Paradise
He lights, and to his proper shape returns
A Seraph wing'd: Six wings he bore to shade
His lineaments divine; the pair that clad
Each shoulder broad came mantling o'er his
*   breast*
With regal ornament; the middle pair
Girt like a starry zone his waist, and round
Skirted his loins and thighs with downy gold
And colours dipp'd in Heaven; the third his
*   feet*
Shadow'd from either heel with feather'd
*   mail,*
Sky tinctured grain. Like Maia's son he stood,
And shook his plumes, that heavenly
*   fragrance fill'd*
The circuit wide. Straight knew him all the
*   bands*
Of Angels under watch, and to his state,
And to his message high, in honour rise;
For on some messages high they guess'd him
*   bound.*
Their glittering tents he pass'd, and now is
*   come*
Into the blissful field, through groves of
*   myrrh,*
And flowering odours, cassia, nard, and balm;
A wilderness of sweets; for Nature here
Wanton'd as in her prime, and play'd at will
Her virgin fancies pouring forth more sweet,
Wild above rule or art, enormous bliss.
               John Milton, Paradise Lost

Tobias and the Archangel Raphael *by Francesco Botticini (c.1446-1497).* Sacristy of the Duomo, Forence.

ABOVE
The Archangel Uriel with Satan Falling, *illustration from a 1794 edition of* Paradise Lost.

The Archangel Uriel

Uriel means 'Fire of God'. Probably belonging to both seraphim and cherubim, he presides over hell and is the angel of repentance, pitiless and savage in his treatment of sinners and blasphemers. He is credited with leading Abraham out of Ur, warning Noah of the flood and rebuking Ezra for questioning the ways of God. He is an interpreter of visions and one of the cherubim who guards the entrance to Paradise and the guardian of the Holy Sepulchre (see pages 64-65 and 68-69).

The Monophysite Churches of Ethiopia and Egypt celebrated his feast day on 28 July. It was believed by many that Uriel was the angel form of the patriarch Jacob after his death. It could be argued that this is either contradicted by the suggestion that Uriel was the angel with whom he himself wrestled or confirmed if it is interpreted as his other self; but it would argue against his role in earlier incidents, though one non-canonical Hebrew text, *The Prayer of Joseph*, has Uriel saying 'I have come down to earth to dwell among men, and I am called by the name of Jacob.'

The Archangel Uriel
His back was turned but not his brightness hid;
Of beaming sunny rays a golden tiar
Circled his head, nor less his locks behind
Illustrious on his shoulders fledge with wings
Lay waving round; on some great charge employ'd
He seemed, or fixed in cogitation deep.
... his radiant visage turn'd,
Admonish'd by his ear, and straight was known

The Archangel Uriel, one of the seven
Who in God's presence, nearest his throne,
Stand ready at command, and are his eyes
That run through all the Heavens, or down to Earth
Bear his swift errands over moist and dry,
O'er sea and land ...'

John Milton, *Paradise Lost*

The Archangel Azrael

Azrael is the Islamic Angel of Death. He has four faces, one on his head, one beneath his feet, one on his front and one on his back, and his body is covered with countless eyes. Every time an eye closes it signifies a death. Michael is sometimes cited as the Christian Angel of Death and rabbinical lore mentions a number, including some evil or fallen angels. Saraquael is one contender, a seraph who is also associated with healing. The idea of an angel covered in eyes continues in at least one other called Sammael, mentioned in the Talmud. A tenth-century scholar, linking Azrael to the angel King David saw threatening Jerusalem, describes an angel formed of yellowish flame, with eyes which shine with bluish fire, and in his hand a drawn sword which he points at the person who is about to die.

An illumination from a medieval manuscript showing Death as a skeletal angel with devil-like wings. This links the angel with the skeletons of the macabre dance-of-death figures which were common at the time of the Black Death and later.

The Angel of Death *by Evelyn de Morgan (1850-1919). This dark and brooding figure of Death is linked with a poem:*

> O Love in Glory
> With crowned brow
> I feel thine arms
> Around me now.
> Soft they kisses
> Warm thy breath
> Vision of love
> Angel of Death.'

The De Morgan Foundation, London.

The Mourning *by George Edgar Hicks (1824-1914). Any sense of harsh judgement or terror at the thought of Death is totally absent from this garnering of a child's soul, full of the sentiment of its period.* Forbes Magazine Collection.

MORTALS INTO ANGELS

High among the ranks of angels are the partriarchs, prophets and saints who are said to have become angels after their deaths. Uriel/Jacob has already been mentioned as an archangel, the others are:

Metatron

Often presented as the highest of all angels. The Talmud describes Metatron as the link between the human and the divine. One of the tallest of all angels, the kabbalists identified him with the pillar of light leading the Israelites out of Egypt in Exodus. Judaic lore suggests this angel to be the angelic form of Enoch, transformed into a spirit of fire having 36 pairs of wings and countless eyes.

Sandalphon

This is the angelic form of the prophet Elijah who at the end of his life was carried off to heaven (see page 31). Some sources suggest that he was already an angel who assumed earthly form. He is sometimes described as the twin of Metatron and is also very tall. The kabbalists thought he had an influence over the sex of unborn children.

Rhamiel

St. Francis not only received the stigmata from a cherub (see pages 74-75), he also became the Angel of Mercy. As the Angel of the Apocalypse he instructs the winds not to complete the destruction of the world until 'the elect should be gathered'.

The Fallen Angels

Where does the evil in the world come from if all creation is the work of God? In the *Book of Isaiah* God declares 'I make peace, and create evil: I the Lord do all these things.' It has been argued that evil must exist to provide choice so that the balance of good can prevail, and to allow the operation of free will and enable good deeds to be recognized. Eve's tempter in the Garden of Eden, the Satan who goads Job and the tempter who appears to Jesus in the Wilderness, can be seen as 'the Adversary' a role similar to that which we now call 'Devil's Advocate', and perhaps with all such bad influences should be seen as 'evil' angels, not necessarily embodying evil in themselves, but a neutral force carrying out God's will by testing his creations. This corresponds with the idea of twinned guardian and evil angels.

Another concept, developed by the Alexandrian theologian Origen, was that angels were creatures of free will and though many at the Creation immediately chose to remain on the side of God, shining with the brightness of celestial beings, those who chose otherwise drifted away, some taking on human form (for Origen proposed that humans could also become angels), those wandering furthest from God becoming purposeless and eventually demons.

The Old Testament describes how '... when men began to multiply on the face of the earth, and daughters were born unto them, that the sons of God saw the daughters of men that they were fair; and they took them wives of all which they chose ...

'There were giants in the earth in those days; and also after that, when the sons of God came in unto the daughters of men, and they bare children to them, the same mighty men which were of old, men of renown.

'And God saw the wickedness of man was great in the earth, and that every imagination of the thoughts of his heart was only evil continually.'

These events which led to God flooding His creation and destroying all life, except that which was gathered on

ABOVE
St. Michael and the Devil *by Jacob Epstein (1880-1959). Sculpted for this location by the entrance to the cathedral at Coventry, built next to the ruins of the one destroyed in the Second World War and a symbol of peace and reconciliation, Satan is seen already vanquished and chained.*

OPPOSITE
The Fall of the Rebel Angels *by Sebastiano Ricci (1659-1734).*
Dulwich Art Gallery, London.

Noah's Ark, could be attributed simply to the fact of human reproduction being tainted with sin, but some interpret the sons of God as meaning angels and in Enoch and some later authorities they are described as being the 'watchers' who came to the aid of the archangels in the creation of Eden. They became overcome with lust for earthly women and descended to earth under their leader Semyaza. Their huge children, 3000 cubits high, not only ate up all that mankind could produce but began to kill both animals and humans, while the giants' offspring, the nephilim, were vicious and harmful by nature.

Meanwhile, the watchers, and especially one called Asael, had begun to teach humanity how to make iron swords and war armour, how to work gold and silver and make jewellery and to use makeup, all of which appear to have been considered sinful.

The Archangel Gabriel is sent to destroy the giants, by setting them against one other so that they destroy themselves; the Archangel Raphael is sent to bind Asael and another called Sariel is sent to find Noah and with the angels help to build the ark.

Enoch, in his vision, is asked by the watchers to plead on their behalf but their plea is rejected and they are hurled down into hell – though they seem since to have managed to escape its limitations and return to earth as devils.

In a second book ascribed to Enoch, the *Book of Secrets*, yet another account is given of the fallen angels, here seen as synonymous with stars, which points to pride rather than lust: the reason for their fall is that their leader wished to set his throne as high as God's and is cast down for his presumption along with his followers who, as they fall, turn into animals:
'And I saw one of those who had first come forward, and he seized the first star that had fallen from heaven and bound it hand and foot and cast it into a pit which was deep and narrow, shut in and dark.

'And one of them drew a sword and gave

it to those elephants and camels and asses and they started to strike each other, their action making the whole earth shake.

'And in my vision, as I watched, behold, one of those that came forward stoned them from heaven, and he took took all those many stars, whose male organs were like those of horses, and gathered them up and bound them all hand and foot, and threw them in a pit of the earth.'

Though their overwheening pride is the chief reason for such retribution, giving rein to their sexuality again appears to be another fault which brings punishment.

This version is alluded to in the *Book of Isaiah* in the fact that Lucifer, Son of Morning, is promised the same fate in very similar language, though the intention here was probably to warn Nebuchadnezzar that God will deal with his presumption in much the same way.

Yet another variation is the concept of a war in heaven between a group of angels who have freely chosen to sin and a group, under the generalship of the Archangel Michael, whom God imbues with His grace and favour. Michael's forces cast the sinful out of heaven but they still survive and will do so until the forces of good win their final victory on the Day of Judgement.

Dante describes the once beautiful angel, now Satan, as a hideous monster trapped in the fourth ring of hell, frozen up to his chest in ice. He has three heads: in front a red one and from the middle of each shoulder and joining at the crown two more, one yellowish white, the other brown like an Ethiopian; six eyes weep and six mouths chew on sinners, dripping blood down his chin. He has three pairs of huge featherless wings, formed like a bat's and beating to create three winds.

Dante names him Dis, Cocytus, Lucifer and Beelzebub, but Satan or Lucifer are the more frequently used to identify hell's ruler, and the other names are often assigned to lesser devils.

If trapped in hell as these images suggest, how is it possible for the fallen angels to perform their devilry on earth? It may be that just as the angels can worship God in heaven, at the same time they to have power to inhabit both spheres at the same time. But then to what purpose is their binding?

John Milton's great poem *Paradise Lost* does not show Satan bound. His is probably the most widely know description of the War in Heaven. Milton

The Fall of the Rebel Angels, *an illumination from* Les Très Riches Heures du Duc de Berry. *The illuminator has not differentiated any of the orders but there are angels missing right through the tiers of heaven, arranged rather like a parliament or conference.* Musée Condé, Chantilly.

first presents Satan, his second-in-command Beelzebub and their rebel angels lying in the fiery lake of hell and in their new-built palace of Pandemonium, debating whether to launch another war to regain heaven. Satan, leaves hell to make a reconnaisance. Like the good angels he is able to assume other forms in order to get past the Archangel Uriel and reach Earth :

'But first he casts to change his proper shape,
Which else might work him danger or delay:
And now a stripling cherub he appears,
Not of the prime, yet such as in his face
Youth smiled celestial, and to every limb
Suitable grace diffused, so well he feign'd;
Under a coronet his flowing hair
In curls on either cheek play'd; wings he wore
Of many a colour'd plume, sprinkled with gold;
His habit fit for speed succinct, and held
Before his decent steps a silver wand.'

In Eden he sees Eve and puts temptation into her mind but is discovered and expelled by guardian angels. Then Archangel Raphael relates to Adam the story of heaven's battles

against Satan, before the world's creation, which were eventually won when the Son of God forces them over the edge of heaven down through chaos to hell.

Satan, returning to Eden enters the body of the serpent and successfully tempts Eve, bringing about the fall of man, and then returns to hell in triumph, while on earth the history of mankind unfolds.

Asael and Semyaza have already been mentioned as leaders of the 'watchers' and Enoch also names Sariel, Rumiel, Danjal, Turel and Kokabiel and several other fallen angels. Judaic tradition adopted the Greek sun god Apollo as the fallen Apollyon or Abbadon as a serpent in the pit. St. Thomas Aquinas equated the fallen angels with demons and as all the gods of heathen religions came to be considered demons in the minds of Christians in the Middle Ages attempts were often made to give them an angelic identity.

In an attempt to match the seven archangels, the following archdemons have been suggested, linked to the seven vices: Lucifer (Pride), Mammon (Avarice), Asmodeus (Lechery), Satan (Anger), Beelzebub (Gluttony), Leviathan (Envy) and Belphegor (Sloth).

The shayatin, the demons of Islam, are quite different. They are a separate form of creature probably equivalent to the ifrit or diabolical spirits of Arabian mythology, which like the demons of the New Testament are credited with being the cause of diseases and accidents. In pre-Islamic times the ifrit were a kind of supernatural spirit known as jinni, along with the ghil, mischievous spirits who can change their shape, and the sila, treacherous spirits who are of fixed form. These are the spirits that dwell in inanimate things, known to Westerners as genies through the stories of *One Thousand and One Nights*, which tease and trick men and women who cross them but can be made use of by those who know the formula for controlling them.

In Islam, however, jinns are spirits, ranked below the angels, which were created 2000 years before God made Adam, as the Qur'an says, 'from the fire of a scorching wind'. They were given reason but are more prone to evil than human creation; some of them worship God and obey him and others do not. A verse of the Qur'an makes it clear that Iblis, the Evil One of Islam who performs the role of the tempter Satan, is one of their number.

It is when the angels are told to bow down before Adam, God's new creation, who has higher rank because he has been given life by the breath of God, that Iblis refuses. His excuse for his disobedience, that to bow would be to transgress against the rule that only God himself shall receive worship, is not accepted.

Satan and the Rebel Angels *by William Blake (1757-1827). Blake shows Satan still in appearance a splendid angel, a reminder that he was once among the highest echelons of heaven.* Victoria and Albert Museum, London.

The Angel with the Key of the Abyss, *woodcut by Albrecht Dürer (1471-1528). This is Apollyon, the Angel of the Bottomless Pit, in the* Book of Revelation *who binds the devil. John Bunyan in* Pilgrim's Progress *gives the name to the devil, and it is often thought to be synonymous with Abaddon, a fallen angel who was said to have regretted his rebellion.*

Angelic Visitations

There are numerous appearances of angels recorded in Scripture and in the stories of the saints and many people claim to have seen them. Whether they can be considered as actual beings from another world, an embodiment of a spirit in human form, a dream vision or a product of the individual mind, must be a matter of interpretation. In depicting such apparitions, artists have usually, but not always, chosen to show angels as conforming to the generally accepted iconography, and have often interpreted the circumstances of the appearance with an imaginative re-creation of the event rather than following the often sparse account given in the Bible.

The following pages present a selection of some of the main angelic visitations and the variety of ways in which artists have interpreted them. Since angels are considered to be ever present, they are often shown even when they have no paricular role in the situation and are not meant to be visible to the human participants. They therefore appear as guardians, watchers and supporters in scenes from the life of Christ and of the saints.

These visitations have been arranged roughly in the sequence of their biblical chronology, not according to the date of the paintings, and where appropriate, are given their scriptural reference. These are followed by pictures associated with later saints and other interpretations of the angelic theme.

In the most famous image of the creation of man, painted by Michelangelo Buonarotti (1475-1564), on the ceiling of the Vatican's Sistine Chapel from 1508-1512, the artist shows the angels massed behind God. They are witnesses to the creation of Adam, fashioned from the earth's clay in the image of God as much as his own. Indeed, very human, naked and without any of the trappings of the angelic form. Vatican Museum, Rome.

THE OLD TESTAMENT
Angels at the Creation and the Fall of Man

The angels were created before man so they were already present to witness the creation of the human race. Jewish tradition suggests that they were created on either the second or the fifth day. Christian belief places the angels above man in the hierarchy of creation – the King James Authorized Version of the Bible translates Psalm 8 thus:

'What is man, that thou art mindful of him? and the son of man, that thou visitest him? For thou has made him a little lower than the angels and hast crowned him with glory and honour. Thou madest him to have dominion over the works of thy hands; thou hast put all things under his feet.'

In the Qur'an, however, God creates Adam as a vice-regent upon the earth. The angels say:

'Wilt thou place therein one who will make Mischief therein and shed blood? Whilst we do celebrate thy praises And glorify Thy holy name?'

The Islamic angel may reflect God's perfection but it has no will of its own, whereas man is given choice. The angels are not imbued with emotion, unlike man whose feelings can both raise him high and drag him into the abyss. They saw only the potential mischief man could make.

Adam is asked to name the creatures of the earth and this in Islam can be interpreted as more than merely naming them but suggests an understanding of the nature of things, which places man nearer to God. That perhaps explains why the angels are then ordered to bow down and honour Adam – an order which Iblis refuses. Iblis appears to be one of the angels and is usually interpreted as Satan, but in a retelling of this incident in a later sura he is described as a jinn.

Islam does not embrace the concept of the fallen angels which is found in Christian tradition, and if this angelic rebellion is placed in the time of Noah (see page 34) it is also impossible for the serpent who successfully persuades Eve to break God's commandment to be a form of fallen angel. Others place the descent of the fallen angels before the Creation.

St. Paul, who seems to have absorbed much of the later Jewish concepts of angels, in his Epistle to the Hebrews, pre-echoes the Qur'anic verses in that God instructs all his angels to worship 'the first begotten into the world', though the reference here may be to Christ rather than man for, unlike Adam and the angels, he was begotten, not created.

In a Turkish manuscript of about 1610, Adam and Eve, having already covered their nakedness, are watched by an angel through the gates of the Garden of Eden. Is the snake, cursed by God for tempting Eve and destined to crawl forever on its belly, Satan, or a being in his control? The Qur'an makes no mention of the serpent, only Satan, but the snake is clearly depicted here. Topkapi Museum, Istanbul.

Abraham and His Family

The patriarch Abraham appears to have been in communication with God either directly or through a vision which promised him the land of Canaan for his descendants, as well as His everlasting protection. But Abraham had no children and his wife Sarah suggested that he beget a child upon her Egyptian servant Hagar. When Hagar became pregnant she began to despise her mistress and Sarah sent her away. To her came an angel, the first angelic messenger identified as such in Scripture.

In a painting from a 15th-century French manuscript of Cas des Nobles Hommes et Femmes, *translated from Boccaccio, Adam and Eve are driven from Eden by an angel. While Adam and his wife sewed fig leaves to cover themselves, God makes them coats of skins before sending Adam forth 'to till the ground'. Genesis says*
'He drove out the man: and he placed at the east of the garden of Eden Cherubims, and a flaming sword which turned every way, to keep the way of the tree of life.' *However, the iconographic tradition usually amalgamates the two and presents an angel, brandishing a sword, driving Adam and Eve from Eden.* Musée Condé, Chantilly.

'And the angel of the Lord found her by a fountain of water in the wilderness, by the fountain in the way to Shur. And he said to Hagar, Sarah's maid, whence camest thou? and wither wilt thou go? and she said, I flee from the face of my mistress Sarah. And the angel of the Lord said unto her, Return to thy mistress, and submit thyself under her hands. And the angel of the Lord said unto her, I will multiply thy seed exceedingly, that it shall not be numbered for multitude. And the angel of the Lord said unto her, Behold thou art with child, and shall bear a son, and shall call him Ishmael: because the Lord hath heard thy affliction. And he will be a wild man; his hand will be against every man, and every man's hand against him; and he shall dwell in the presence of all his brethren.

And she called the name of the Lord that spake unto her, Thou God seest me: for she said, Have I also here looked after him that seeth me?'

When Ishmael was 13 years old, God made his Covenant with Abraham, instructing that he and the males of his household, and in future all boys when they became eight days old, should be circumcised. So Hagar's son became one of the first to follow this rite.

Ishmael is especially important in Islam, both for his part in the original Covenant with God and because the Arab Nation was descended from him.

On a later occasion, three men appeared outside Abraham's tent, one of whom Abraham realized was God, the others presumably being angels. God now told him that, despite their age and that Sarah was barren and no longer menstruated, they would have a son. He also told him that He planned to destroy the cities of Sodom and Gomorrah for their sinfulness. When Abraham begged Him not to destroy the righteous with the wicked, He agreed to spare them if he could find ten men that were virtuous.

Abraham's nephew Lot was at Sodom and there two angels appeared whom he welcomed into his house. The men of the city gathered round the house demanding to see the strangers and asked Lot to bring them out 'that we may know them'. Lot, interpreting this to mean sexual congress, and believing the laws of hospitality to be paramount, offered his daughters in their place only to be threatened himself. The angels blinded the men and instructed Lot and his family to flee the city before it was destroyed. They were warned that in no

In an illustration to a 15th century French manuscript illuminated by the Boucicaut Master and workshop. God, wearing a papal style tiara, presents Eve to Adam. They are surrounded by the animals of the Garden of Eden, which is enclosed by a wattle fence. Over it watch both red six-winged seraphim and ordinary angels, one of which has a sword. Bibliothèque Nationale, Paris.

BELOW
Abraham with the Three Angels by Giovanni Domenico Tiepolo (1727-1804). It seems hardly likely that Abraham would have thought these were three ordinary travellers turning up outside his tent, but this is no doubt intended to be the moment when the patriarch recognizes his God in the beautiful naked figure. Galleria dell'Accademia, Venice.

circumstance must they look back. So Lot and his daughters escaped the destruction of Sodom and Gomorrah, but his wife looked back and was turned immediately into a pillar of salt.

God had not forgotten his promise of a son for Sarah and Abraham and He 'did unto Sarah as He had spoken', and so Isaac was born when Abraham was well over 100 years old. Sarah resented the presence of Ishmael, his half brother, and Hagar and Ishmael were again sent away. They crossed the desert and ran out of water and Hagar, unable to bear watching her son die of thirst, sat a distance away from him and wept:

'and the Angel of God called to Hagar out of heaven, and said unto her, What aileth thee Hagar? Fear not: for God hath heard the voice of the lad where he is. Arise, lift up the lad, and hold him in thine hand; for I will make him a great nation. And God opened her eyes, and she saw a well of water; and she went, and filled the bottle with water, and gave the lad drink. And God was with the lad: and he grew, and dwelt in the wilderness, and became an archer.'

God now demanded that Abraham make a sacrifice of Isaac and he obediently made preparation and took his son to the place appointed binding him upon the altar. He was about to strike with a knife to kill his son when

'the angel of the Lord called unto him out of heaven, and said, Abraham, Abraham; and he said, Here am I. And he said, Lay not thine hand upon the lad, neither do thou any thing unto him: for now I know that thou fearest God, seeing thou hast not withheld thy son, thine only son from me.

And Abraham lifted up his eyes, and looked, and beheld behind him a ram caught in a thicket by his horns; and Abraham went and took the ram, and offered him up for a burnt offering in the stead of his son.'

Moslems believe that this sacrifice took place before the birth of Isaac and that the intended offering was Ishmael, since God asks Abraham to take his *only* son, and that Ishmael offered himself as a willing victim.

Lot and his Daughters leaving Sodom *by Louis de Caullery (c. 1580-1621). While one angel leads Lot and another his daughters, their mother stands behind them, turned to salt. The angels appear to have already completed their mission of destruction.* Rafael Valls Gallery, London.

Jacob's Dream

Abraham's chief steward found Isaac a wife, Rebekah, with angelic help and they had twin sons Esau and Jacob. Jacob cheated Esau out of his inheritance as the eldest son and avoiding his brother's wrath and seeking a wife, leaves Canaan and halting on his journey

' ... tarried there all night, because the sun was set; and he took of the stones of that place, and put them for his pillows, and lay down in that place to sleep. And he dreamed, and behold a ladder set up on the earth, and the top of it reached to heaven: and behold the angels of God ascending and descending on it. And behold the Lord stood above it, and said, I am the Lord God of Abraham ... '

Afterwards Jacob made an offering to God and promised his worship if he could have God's support.

Later he told his wives, gained by hard toil from their father, that an angel had appeared to him and showed him speckled and patched cattle, those of their father's flock which were to be his – patterns which he achieved by making them mate by bark-stripped willow

Hagar in the Desert *by Pompeo Batoni (1708-1787). Ishmael lies weak and dying, an empty pitcher by his side, while his distraught mother has torn her garments. The fountain gushes forth as though the angel has just brought it into being.* Galleria Nazionale d'Arte Antica, Rome.

In a Turkish painting of 1583, the angel brings the ram for sacrifice instead of Ishmael (or Isaac). (See also page 44). Museum of Turkish and Islamic Arts.

wands – and told him to return to Canaan. On the way, much troubled as to whether his twin would accept his return he sends his family, flocks and servants across a ford, remaining on the other bank.

'And Jacob was left alone; and there wrestled a man with him until the breaking of the day. And when he saw that he prevailed not against him, he touched the hollow of his thigh; and the hollow of Jacob's thigh was out of joint, as he wrestled with him. And he said let me go for the day breaketh. And he said, I will not let thee go, except thou bless me. And he said, Let me go, for the day breaketh. And he said, I will not let thee go, except thou bless me. And he said unto him, What is thy name? And he said, Jacob. And he said, Thy name shall be called no more Jacob, but Israel: for as a prince hast thou power with God and with men, and hast prevailed. And Jacob asked him, and said, Tell me, I pray thee, thy name. And he said, Wherefore is it that thou dost ask after my name? And he blessed him there.'

The man is usually considered to have been an angel, or can be interpreted as a metaphor for the moral struggle that was going on in Jacob's mind.

Abraham's Sacrifice *by Harmensz van Rijn Rembrandt (1606-1669). Only Isaac's hands are bound behind his back and his father has his hand over his son's face so that he shall not see the blow he is about to strike. Then the angel appears. It hs been suggested that Rembrandt's wife Saskia may have been the model for the angel.* Hermitage, Leningrad.

OPPOSITE PAGE
Jacob's Ladder *by William Blake (1757-1827). Blake shows both angels and human beings using this great spiral stair. The idea of the ladder as a means of access between heaven and earth probably pre-dates the concept of angels having wings to fly between them.* British Library, London.

ABOVE
Detail from the Fight between Jacob and the Angel *by Eugene Delacroix (1798-1863).* Church of Ste-Sulpice, Paris

Moses and the Exodus

To Moses, an angel appeared in the form of a flaming bush and spoke with the voice of God. He instructed him to go to Pharaoh and to lead the people of Israel out of Egypt. The Exodus text does not involve angels in God's communication with Moses instructing him in his dealings with Pharaoh, saying simply that God spoke to him. In the same way, the seven plagues unleashed against Egypt are brought about by God, as well as the killing of the Egyptian firstborn. In order that Jewish households were exempted from this massacre, they killed a sacrificial lamb, marking their doorposts with its blood and performed other acts ordered by God which are still celebrated in the rituals of the Passover. The text says that 'seeing the blood upon the lintel, and on the two side posts, the Lord will pass over the door, and will not suffer the destroyer to come in'. The destroyer may be a metaphor for death but most people,

and artists certainly, visualize this as the Angel of Death, and we may imagine that angels played a very active role in the spreading of all the plagues of Egypt.

To lead them out of Egypt there was an angel with, or in the form of, a pillar of cloud to go bright before them, at times moving behind them to hide them from pursuing Egyptian forces. In his communications throughout the Exodus through the desert into Canaan (including the giving of the Ten Commandments), God continues to speak directly to Moses, though again sending an angel to guide him.

Balaam and His Ass

Balaam was a diviner and enchanter whom the King of Moab hoped to persuade to put a curse on Moses and the Israelites who had fought their way through to his territory. When the king's messengers arrived, God told Balaam to refuse to go to the king and perform the

Israelites Passing Through the Wilderness *by William West (1801-1861). The angel leads Moses and his people in the form of a pillar of light. Below his brightness, the Ark of the Covenant is carried before the people.* City of Bristol Museum and Art Gallery.

curse for him; but when they came a second time he went, taking two servants with him. But an angel came to stop them:

'... and the ass saw the angel of the Lord standing in the way and his sword drawn in his hand; and the ass turned aside out of the way, and went into the field, and Balaam smote the ass, to turn her into the way. But the angel of the Lord stood in a part of the vineyards, a wall being on this side, and a wall on that side. And when the ass saw the angel of the Lord, she thrust herself unto the wall, and crushed Balaam's foot against the wall: and he smote her again. And the angel of the Lord went further and stood in a narrow place, where there was no way to turn either to the right or to the left. And when the ass saw the angel of the Lord she fell down under Balaam: and Balaam's anger was kindled and he smote the ass with a staff. And the Lord opened the mouth of the ass, and she said to Balaam, What have I done unto thee, that thou hast smitten me these three times? And*

Balaam said unto the ass, Because thou hast mocked me: I would there were a sword in mine hand, for now would I kill thee. And the ass said unto Balaam, Am I not thine ass, upon which thou hast ridden ever since I was thine unto this day? Was I ever wont to do so unto thee? And he said, Nay.

Then the Lord opened the eyes of Balaam, and he saw the angel of the Lord standing in the way, and his sword drawn in his hand: and he bowed down his head, and fell flat on his face.'*

The angel instructs Balaam to go to the king but only to do as God instructs him. Balaam has the king build seven altars and make offerings and then asks why he should curse where God has not cursed and instead he blesses Israel.

Kings and Prophets

The Bible usually presents God as communicating directly with the leaders and prophets of the Israelites. However, an angel is sent to Joshua by the walls of

Balaam's Ass by Hans Bol (1534-593). The donkey has seen the angel and fallen in fright long before its master is aware of it. Bol has taken the essence of the successive actions of the angel, ignoring the described locations and making the donkey fall at the first sighting.

Jericho, declaring himself to be captain of the hosts of the Lord and another appears at Bochim speaking on God's behalf and rebuking his people for not obeying his instructions to destroy altars to local gods and avoid alliances with local peoples. It is an angel who summons Gideon to leadership, that tells another childless woman that she will give birth to Samson, and it is an angel that spreads pestilence in the days of King David. Satan is credited with giving David the idea of counting his subjects and incurring God's wrath thereby (ours not to reason why), and when an angel is sent to destroy Jerusalem, David sees it stand between the earth and the heaven, a drawn sword in his hand stretched out over Jerusalem. An angel brings food and water to Elijah in the wilderness which sustains him for 40 days and nights and angels instruct him in his dealings with the King of Samaria. Elijah, himself, ascended to heaven in a chariot of fire (see page 31) and, according to a later tradition, himself became an angel.

In the time of the prophet Isaiah, an angel is said to have destroyed the army of the Assyrian king Sennacharib but in the book of the Bible which bears Isaiah's name, a vision of heaven is described which gives some specific information about the angels, as later do the visions of Ezekiel and Zachariah.

The *Book of Job* introduces Satan as the evil angel, that is an angel sent to bring about evil on God's instruction, but God speaks to Job not through another angel but through a whirlwind.

The *Book of Daniel* also speaks of the attendants around the throne of God and, although it is Daniel who interprets the dreams of Nebuchadnezzar and Belshazzar, it is an angel who appears within Daniel's own visions to explain them to him. One of Nebuchadnezzar's dreams seems to involve an angel: 'a watcher and an holy one'. In reality, rather than dreams, Daniel records the refusal of three Jewish administrators in Babylon to worship a huge gold image set up on the plain of Dura. In punishment these three, Shadrach, Meshach and Abednego are thrown into a furnace: *'Then Nebuchadnezzar the king was astonished, and rose up in haste, and spake, and said unto his counsellors, Did not we cast three men bound into the midst of the fire? They answered and said, True, O king. He answered and said, Lo, I see four men loose,*

TOP
Elijah Visited by an Angel *by Alessandro Bonvicino Moretto Da Brescia (1498-1554). An angel brings cake and water to the prophet on two occasions, thus providing him with enough sustenance to survive for a further 40 days in the wilderness.* Church of San Giovanni Evangelista, Brescia.

ABOVE
An Angel Destroys the Assyrians, *a coloured woodcut from the Nuremberg Bible of 1483 (Biblia Sacra Germanica).* Victoria and Albert Museum, London.

walking in the midst of the fire, and they have no hurt; and the form of the fourth is like the Son of God.

Then Nebuchadnezzar came near to the mouth of the burning fiery furnace, and spake, and said, Shadrach, Meshach, and Abednego, ye servants of the most high God, come forth, and come hither. Then Shadrach, Meshach and Abednego, came forth of the midst of the fire.'

The fourth figure is an angel.

Later, officials and politicians jealous of Daniel's position in the kingdom, persuade Darius to ban for 30 days the petitioning of any god or man except the king himself. In this way they trap Daniel whom they know very well will go on praying to his God and Daniel is thrown into the lions' den:

'Now the king spake and said unto Daniel, thy God whom thou servest continually, he will deliver thee. And a stone was brought and laid upon the mouth of the den; and the king sealed it with his own signet.

Then the king arose next morning, and went in haste unto the den of lions. And when he came to the den, he cried with a lamentable voice unto Daniel: and the king spake and said to Daniel, O Daniel, servant of the living God, is thy God, whom thou servest continually, able to deliver thee from the lions?

Then said Daniel unto the king, O my king, live for ever. My God hath sent his angel, and hath shut the lions' mouths, and they have not hurt me; as much as before him innocence was found in me; and also before thee O king, have I done no hurt.'

Daniel in the Lions' Den, *an illumination from a manuscript of a commentary on the Apocalypse by the 8th-century Spanish monk Beatus de Liebana, illuminated by monks at the Benedictine monastery at Silos in northern Spain between 1091-1109. British Library.*

Tobias and the Angel

The *Book of Tobit* is part of the Roman Catholic Bible although excluded from the Jewish and Protestant canonical texts. It purports to be written by a devout Jew, one of those taken as captives to Nineveh, in the seventh century B.C. The known text is thought to date from about 175-164 B.C. Antioch when those Jews faithful to their religion were not allowed to bury their dead. Tobit himself does just this in defiance of the local authority.

The story goes that Tobit, sleeping outside his house because he is now ritually polluted by the burial, is blinded by bird-droppings. At the same time Sarah, a young woman of Ecbatana, seven-times married, whose husbands have all been killed by a demon called Asmodeus before any of the marriages have been consummated, wishes to have a husband. Both Tobit and Sarah pray to God for help.

Tobit asks his son Tobias to go to Media to collect a sum of money which he had left with a man there, but asks him to find an escort to travel with him. Tobias choses a man who calls himself Azarias, who is actually the Archangel Raphael. When Tobias goes to wash in the River Tigris, a great fish leaps from the water big enough to swallow him, but Azarias tells him to grasp the fish and he hauls it onto land. Then he tells Tobias to cut out its heart, liver and gall and wrap them up before they cook and eat the fish, explaining that smoke from the heart and liver will drive off an evil spirit and that the gall will 'cure whiteness of the eyes'.

On their journey Azarias speaks to him about Sarah and says that they must marry, and that the fish smoke will protect him from the spirit Asmodeus. So when they reach Sarah's home Tobias marries her and putting the heart and liver on the embers of an incense burner foils the devil that comes to kill him. While his wife's parents insist he stay there to celebrate the marriage feast, Azarias collects the money and afterwards they all return to Tobit, using the fish gall to restore his sight. Tobit and Tobias then insist that for his help Azarias have half the money he had collected and only then does Raphael reveal himself as 'one of the seven holy angels, which present the prayers of the saints, and which go in and out before the glory of the Holy One.'

Tobit is said to be 85 years old when he loses his sight and blind for eight years before Tobias restores it, by rubbing the gall of the fish on his eyes, and he lives to the age of 185. After both parents die Tobias, Sarah and their family go back to Ecbatana where he in turn lives to 127.

BELOW
Tobias and the Angel by Jean-Charles Cazin (1814-1901). This treatment by a more recent French artist omits his dog and the great fish but has a much more believable youth as Tobias instead of the small boy so often shown in Renaissance paintings of the subject.

Meanwhile, Nineveh is destroyed.

Tobias does not necessarily take a companion because he is young but because travel is safer when accompanied. However, artists nearly always show him as a boy or very young man. He is accompanied by his dog, mentioned in the scriptural text, and carries a whole fish, despite the fact that it was eaten on the riverside and only its offal removed from the scene. Botticini, in a painting now in the Uffizi Gallery, adds the Archangels Michael and Gabriel and gives Raphael peacock's feather wings.

OPPOSITE
Tobias and the Archangel Raphael *by a follower of Titian (c.1485-1576).* Galleria dell'Accademia, Venice.

THE GOSPELS

As with the patriarchs of the Old Testament an angel, identified this time as Gabriel, appeared to tell Zacharias, an elderly and childless priest of Israel in the days when Herod was king of Judea, that his barren wife Elizabeth will have a child. Because he failed to believe the angel, Zacharias was struck dumb until the boy, John the Baptist, was born and he had named him. When Elizabeth was six month's pregnant Gabriel appeared in Nazareth, a city of Galilee, to her cousin Mary, a virgin soon to be married. St. Luke's Gospel tells what he said:

'Hail thou that art highly favoured, the Lord is with thee: blessed art thou among women. And when she saw him, she was troubled at his saying, and cast in her mind what manner of salutation this should be. And the angel said unto her, Fear not, Mary: for thou hast found favour with God. And, behold, thou shalt conceive in thy womb, and bring forth a son, and shall call his name Jesus. He shall be great, and shall be called the Son of the Highest: and the Lord God shall give unto him the throne of his father David: And he shall reign over the house of Jacob for ever; and of his kingdom there shall be no end.

Then said Mary unto the angel, How shall this be, seeing I know not a man? And the angel answered and said unto her: The Holy Ghost shall come upon thee, and the power of the Highest shall overshadow thee: therefore also that holy thing which shall be born of thee shall be called the Son of God. And, behold, thy cousin Elizabeth, she hath also conceived a son in her old age: and this is the sixth month with her, who was called barren. For with God nothing shall be impossible.

And Mary said, Behold the handmaid of the Lord: be it unto me according to thy word. And the angel departed from her.'

This scene, the Annunciation, has been painted by many artists and was especially popular with the development of devotion to the Mother of God along with those which show her as the Madonna with the infant Jesus.

St. Matthew's Gospel describes the reaction of Joseph when

'... before they came together, she was found with child of the Holy Ghost. Then Joseph her husband, being a just man, and not willing to make a publick example, was minded to put her away privily. But while he thought on these things, behold, the angel of the Lord appeared unto him in a dream, saying, Joseph, thou son of David, fear not to take unto thee Mary they wife: for that which is conceived in her is of the Holy Ghost. And she shall bring forth a son, and thou shalt call his name Jesus: for he shall save his people from their sins.'

The Nativity and After

At Jesus's birth, it may be that the star which led the wise men to the Christ child could be considered a form of angelic apparition and that it was an angel in a dream who told them not to return to Herod and tell him where to find the newborn baby Jesus. Luke reports an angel bringing news of the birth to shepherds outside Bethlehem

'... abiding in the field, keeping watch over their flocks by night. And, lo, the angel of the Lord came upon them, and the glory of the Lord shone round about them: and they were sore afraid.

And the angel said unto them, Fear not: for, behold, I bring you good tidings of great joy, which shall be to all people. For unto you is born this day in the city of David a Saviour, which is Christ the Lord. And this shall be a sign unto you; Ye shall find the babe wrapped in swaddling clothes, lying in a manger.

And suddenly there was with the angel a multitude of the heavenly host praising God, and saying, Glory to God in the highest, and on earth peace, good will toward men.

And it came to pass, as the angels were gone away from them into heaven, the shepherds said one to another, Let us now go even unto Bethlehem, and see this thing which is come to pass, which the Lord hath made known unto us.'

The scene of the Nativity, so popular a subject for paintings, is often presented with angels in attendance. Though there is no scriptural reference to them, except to the angel that appears to Joseph to warn him to leave Bethlehem and flee to Egypt to avoid the massacre of the innocents which Herod orders in the hope of removing this prophesied King of the Jews. Later, after Herod's death, an angel in a dream tells Joseph that it is safe to return.

The Annunciation is a simple confrontation between the angel Gabriel and the Virgin Mary and the emphasis is usually placed upon the protagonists. It is one scene where we always know which angel it is and the white lily, symbol of Mary's purity, which Gabriel frequently carries or which appears prominently in the picture, has become a symbol for identifying Gabriel on other occasions. For other examples of the Angel of the Annunciation see pages 26-29.

The Annunciation *by Jacopo Tintoretto (1518-1594). Unusually for this subject, though they often appear in other biblical scenes, Tintoretto's angel trails flights of little cherubs. He places Mary already in Joseph's house, with the carpenter at work outside.* Scuola Grande di San Rocco, Venice.

LEFT
The Birth of the Virgin Mary *by Albrecht Altdorfer (1480-1538). Mary's birth is not described in Scripture but with increased devotion to the Virgin and the development of the dogma of her Immaculate Conception (the idea that she was conceived without any stain of original sin, not promulgated as dogma until the 19th century), it began to form a subject of some importance. Here, as was frequent in his work, the artist has placed the domestic scene of the birth chamber within a setting of ecclesiastical architecture. The circle of little angels both praise her and emphasize her innocence, sanctified by the censer of the central angel.* Pinakothek, Munich.

St. Joseph and the Angel *by Georges de La Tour (1593-1652). This angel takes entirely human and definitely female form to appear in a dream to Joseph, or is this the pregnant Mary that we see, about to wake Joseph from the dream in which he receives his angelic message.* Wrightsman Collection, New York.

The Annunciation to the Shepherds *by Nicolaes Berchem (1610-1683). The elderly shepherd and the young mother with her baby echo the angel's message while the mixed herd of sheep, goats and cattle is perhaps a reminder that the message is of peace to all men.* City of Bristol Museum and Art Gallery.

The Christ Child Adored by Angels *by
Hugo van der Goes (c.1440-1482), the central
panel of the Portinari altarpiece of 1475. The
shepherds, seen in the background and fright-
ened by the appearance of an angel have
reached the stable of the Nativity. One has
brought his bagpipes to play for the infant.
Their spades would be useful for digging out
sheep from winter snows but also suggest a
wider range of countrymen, working people
balancing the kingship of the Magi and the
glory of the Church which is reflected in the
rich ecclesiastical garments of several of the
angels. Galleria degli Uffizi, Florence.*

Adoration of the Magi *by Andrea*
Mantegna (1428-1506), detail from an
altarpiece. Watched over by angels from
above, the Madonna and Child are encircled
by cherubim and seraphim, the cherubim
being treated in the earlier tradition of
colouring them red. Galleria degli Uffizi,
Florence.

LEFT
The Flight into Egypt *by Marco Meloni (16th century). Although flat-chested the breast bands of the angel suggest that it is female and the direct gaze and exposed leg are somewhat provocative in contrast to the demure Madonna.* Roy Miles Gallery, London.

ABOVE
The Flight into Egypt by *François Verwilt (1620-1691). Painted a century later than Meloni's picture, the single angel has become a host of little putti to accompany the Christ child; the group tormenting the goat is reminiscent of classical subjects but it has been included to suggest an evil force against which they provide protection.* Johnny van Haeften Gallery, London.

The Life of Christ

Apart from the appearance of Satan to tempt Christ in the wilderness, of angels to minister to Him afterwards, and Jesus's own few references to angels and devils in his ministry, angels do not appear again in the scriptural narrative until the time of Christ's Passion. There were, however, incidents where Jesus drove out devils from the sick (at that time many believed that illness was caused by demonic possession), and there is the incident of the angel who disturbed the waters of the Pool of Bethesda where Jesus is asked to perform a healing: but they are few and far between. Nevertheless, since angels were considered to be ever present, watching and guarding, they frequently appear in depictions of any episode from the life of Christ.

As described in the *Book of Job*, the tempting of Jesus by Satan, after He had fasted for forty days and nights, in which Satan is described as a devil, should perhaps be seen not as a personification of evil but as an angel working on God's behalf. Both Matthew and Luke recount this story. This is Matthew's version, beginning when Jesus is hungry from his fast:

'And when the tempter came to him, he said, If thou be the Son of God, command that these stones be made bread. But he answered and said, It is written, Man shall not live by bread alone, but by every word that proceedeth out of the mouth of God.

Then the devil taketh him up into the holy city, and setteth him on a pinnacle of the temple. And saith unto him, If thou be the Son of God, cast thyself down: for it is written, He shall give his angels charge concerning thee: and in their hands they shall bear thee up, lest at any time thou dash thy foot against a stone.

RIGHT

The Baptism of Christ *by Francesco Albani (1571-1660). The ministering angels which attend to Jesus are given a practical role in having ready a towel and clothing.* Phillips, London.

LEFT

St. Joseph and the Christ Child *by El Greco (Domenikos Theotocopoulos 1541-1614). The two tumbling naked angels are close in style to putti. St. Joseph has been given a shepherd's crook, a symbol of his nurturing care of Jesus.* Toledo Cathedral.

Jesus said unto him, It is written again, Thou shalt not tempt the Lord thy God.

Again, the devil taketh him up into an exceeding high mountain, and sheweth him all the kingdoms of the world, and the glory of them. And saith unto him, All these things will I give thee, if thou wilt fall down and worship me.

Then saith Jesus unto him, Get thee hence, Satan: for it is written, Thou shalt worship the Lord thy God, and Him only shalt thou serve.

Then the devil leaveth him, and behold, angels came and ministered unto Him.'

ABOVE
The Third Temptation *by William Blake (1757-1827). Even as Satan, the angel adversary, tempts Jesus there are guardian or ministering angels watching.* Victoria and Albert Museum, London.

ABOVE RIGHT
The Agony in the Garden *by Francisco Jose de Goya (1746-1828). The 'cup' which Jesus asks to be taken from him is metaphorical but often shown as physical in paintings and presented by an angel.*

FAR RIGHT
The Agony in the Garden *by Andrea Mantegna (c. 1428-1506). The group of cherubs are in marked contrast to the compassionate angel shown by so many artists.* National Gallery, London

Christ's Passion and Resurrection

Although not mentioned in the Gospel texts, angels are frequently included in pictures dealing with Christ's Passion. They are occasionally included in depictions of the Last Supper and more frequently in paintings of the Crucifixion. Angels were not thought to possess the gift of foreknowledge which was sometimes given to human prophets and were not to know that these tragic events were necessary preliminaries to a glorious resurrection. Although traditional understanding was that angels had no

emotions, they are often shown reacting to the Passion with great grief, especially in Fra Angelico's paintings in the Arena Chapel, Padua. This could be seen as a case where the circumstances are so harrowing that even the most hard-hearted must feel or, if angels are merely the messengers and transmitters of God's will, they could very well be expressing His own pain and anguish.

With the Resurrection, angels are specifically mentioned in the Gospel texts, though the accounts all differ. St. John describes Mary Magdalene and some of the disciples finding the empty sepulchre in which Jesus was buried. Mary,

returning when the others had departed, saw two angels sitting at the slab, where Jesus had lain, who spoke to her before Jesus himself appeared. Luke reports Mary Magdalene, Mary the mother of James, Joanna and other women seeing two men in shining garments at the tomb; Mark describes the two Marys and a woman called Salome seeing a young man 'in a long white garment'. Matthew gives the fullest account, with only Mary Magdalene and 'the other Mary' arriving at the sepulchre at dawn to anoint the body of Christ:

'And, behold, there was a great earthquake: for the angel of the Lord descended from heaven,

and came and rolled back the stone from the door, and sat upon it. His countenance was like lightning, and his raiment white as snow. And for fear of him the keepers did shake, and became as dead men.

And the angel answered and said unto the women, Fear not ye: for I know that ye seek Jesus, which was crucified. He is not here: for he is risen, as he said. Come, see the place where the Lord lay. And go quickly, and tell his disciples that he is risen from the dead; and, behold, he goeth before you into Galilee; there shall ye see him: lo, I have told you.'

The watch, which Matthew mentions as being the chief priest's responsibility,

are traditionally presented as Roman soldiers, placed there to prevent the followers of Jesus from stealing his body and declaring a false resurrection. None of the canonical gospels describes the group of woman as the 'Three Marys' though tradition has accepted them and they are what most artists have depicted.

Some artists have shown angels as travellers with the group whom the resurrected Jesus joins on the road to Emmaus, attendent at later appearances before the disciples, and of course, at the scene of the Ascension of Christ into heaven, where they often carry Jesus upwards.

The Crucifixion with the Angels *by Charles Lebrun (1619-1690). The foreground figure, offering himself and his crown to Christ, is the young Louis XIV, King of France, and the picture was painted for his mother Anne of Austria c. 1660.* Musée du Louvre, Paris.

The Lamentation of Christ *by Jean Daret (1613-1668). A ministering angel supports the dead Christ before the mourning Virgin and the Magdalene.* Musée des Beaux-Arts, Marseilles.

The Lamentation of Christ *by Ambrogio Bondone Giotto (c. 1266-1337). In this fresco the angels seem even more racked with anguish then the human mourners.* Scrovegni (Arena) Chapel, Padua.

RIGHT
Detail of above.

ABOVE LEFT
The Marys at the Sepulchre, *an illumination from the* Shaftesbury Psalter, *painted in the west of England c. 1130-50.* British Library, London.

LEFT
The Three Marys at Christ's Grave *by H. and J. van Eyck (c. 1370-1426 and 1390-1441). Women, angel, tomb and sleeping soldiers reflect the self-same moment some two-and-half centuries later than when the preceding manuscript illustration was painted.* Museum Buyman-van Beuningen, Rotterdam.

APOSTLES, MARTYRS AND SAINTS

The record of the Acts of the Apostles, usually thought to have been written by St. Luke, does not contain many angelic visitations, although there are references to angels in a more general sense. The first dramatic appearance is when an angel releases the apostles who have been imprisoned by the High Priest's guards. An angel appeared to the disciple Philip (known as the Deacon) telling him to go to Gaza. On the way Philip met an eunuch from the Ethiopian court – whom he converted and baptized – the first Ethiopian Christian, after which the angel reappeared and sent Philip elsewhere.

It is Jesus himself, rather than an angel, who appeared to Saul of Tarsus on the road to Damascus, converting him from a persecutor of Christians into an ardent believer; but an angel appeared to a centurion in Caesarea called Cornelius and told him to send for the apostle Peter, leading to his preaching in Caesarea and the gifts of tongues being bestowed on the disciples at Pentecost.

Peter having been thrown into gaol by Herod, is again released by an angel: ' ... *he was sleeping between two chains: and the keepers before the door kept the prison. And, behold, the angel of the Lord came upon him, and a light shined in the prison: and he smote Peter on the side, and raised him up, saying, Arise up quickly. And his chains fell off from his hands.*

And the angel said unto him, Gird thyself, and bind on thy sandals. And so he did. And he saith unto him, Cast thy garment about thee, and follow me. And he went out,

The Morning of the Resurrection *by Edward Burne-Jones (1833-1898). The angels still wait at the tomb as the risen Christ appears.* Christie's, London.

and followed him: and wist not that it was true which was done by the angel: but thought he saw a vision.

When they were past the first and the second ward, they came unto the iron gate that leadeth unto the city; which opened to them of his own accord: and they went out, and passed on through one street; and forthwith the angel departed from him.'

Soon after St. Peter's escape, an angel is credited with the death of King Herod.

Later, when St. Paul is being shipped to Rome for trial, an angel appears to him on board ship to tell him not to be afraid.

Shortly before his death by stoning the first martyr, Stephen, had a vision of Christ, and declared this to the people. There was no way St. Luke could know what Stephen actually saw as he faced death, but artists have often chosen to present him with angels welcoming him and ready to carry him to heaven. Later, martyrs and saints experiencing visions or performing acts of healing are often shown as watched, helped and guided by angels when incidents from their lives have been depicted.

As in the Bible, angels have appeared in later centuries to religious mystics and pious laymen and sometimes to seemingly ordinary people too, such as the farm girl Jeanne d'Arc from Domrémy who, from about 12 years old, heard voices and saw a piercing light which on

many later occasions resolved into the winged and glorious image of the Archangel Michael, surrounded by glittering angels. He appeared as many as three times a week telling her that she must be pious and good 'for great things are expected of you', until he told her that in future it would be St. Margaret and St. Catherine who would appear to guide her.

This girl, herself to be canonized five centuries later, led the French army to victory against the English in the 15th century.

Armies have always called upon their gods for help in time of war and the enlisting of heavenly support against their enemies was what the Israelites categorically expected from their worship of the God of Abraham and Moses; indeed, the Old Testament records many victories due to heavenly intervention.

In Christian times, the fact that opposing forces have worshipped the same God has not prevented them from claiming that God was on their side or believing His saints and angels fought for them in particular. Just as Joan believed that God was against the English (who when she fell into their hands set about destroying her as a witch in league with the devil), armies throughout the centuries have sought for signs to prove that God was in sympathy with their cause. Even in the First World War British

The Immaculate Conception *by José Antolinez (1635-1675). The idea that from her conception the Virgin Mary was especially privileged to be free of any taint of Original Sin had been current for centuries before it was made an item of Catholic dogma in 1854. During the Middle Ages, this was a subject of contentious debate: the Dominican Order opposed the concept, the Franciscans endorsed and defended it, but in 1476, December 8 was widely celebrated as the Feast of the Immaculate Conception and from the 16th century onwards it was accepted by most of the Catholic Church. A popular subject for devotional paintings, the halo of stars and the innocent looking cherubs emphasize her purity.* Prado, Madrid.

The Assumption of the Virgin Mary *by Paolo (Calliari) Veronese (c. 1528-1588) The Assumption is not an incident of Scripture, though a tradition developed early in the Roman Church that at her death the Mother of God was taken up into heaven, body and soul. It became dogma in 1950, but had long been a frequent subject for religious paintings. Here she is greeted by saints and prophets and every kind of angel around the Heavenly Father.* Galleria dell'Accademia, Venice.

St. Margaret of Antioch by *Charles Joseph Natoire (1700-1777). This legendary virgin martyr was the daughter of the Prince of Antioch. Brought up in the countryside by a nurse who was a secret Christian, she was seen herding sheep by the governor of Antioch who fell in love and wished to marry her. She refused him because by that time she too had become a Christian. While being tortured in prison before her martyrdom, a dragon appeared and swallowed her, but she blessed herself and a mystic cross appeared, piercing the dragon and releasing her, which was interpreted as an angel with a spear. Though she became the patron saint of childbirth, with a dragon as her symbol, she was removed from the list of official saints by the Vatican in 1969.* Phillips, London.

The Ascent of the Prophet Muhammed to Heaven, *an illumination in a 16th-century Persian manuscript by Aqa Mirak. This is the occasion of the Prophet's 'Night Journey'. His face is obscured by a veil for many Moslems would consider it blasphemous to* attempt to depict him: *though portraits do appear in Persian and Turkish Islamic art. His mount Buraq is shown as part angel and part mule. He is accompanied by the angel Jibra'il (or Gabriel) and other attendant angels.* British Library, London.

The Vision of St. Teresa *by Jacopo Amigoni (c. 1682-1752). The Spanish Carmelite nun, founder of convents, who wrote about her mystical experiences, had a vision in which an angel wounded her in the heart with a flaming spear, a symbol of the love of God and His mystical marriage to the nun as Bride of Christ. The painter has avoided the semblance of sexual ecstasy so strong in Bernini's well known sculpture of the subject in Rome.* Phillips, London.

The Angels of Mons *by W.H. Margetson. Was this a vision or a mass hallucination which occurred at the first battle of the First World War in which the British infantry faced German forces – or was it a British propaganda exercise?*

riflemen at the first British encounter with the enemy at the Battle of Mons in August 1914 were said to have seen the white shadowy figures of angels standing between the British lines and the advancing German forces. On 8 September, the story was reported as already current among members of II Corps who had been involved in this action which at first had some success and then turned into a rout: so explanations that it developed from a story published some weeks later can be discounted. There were also figures of archers (echoing the bowmen at Agincourt five centuries earlier) and of phantom horsemen who defended the flanks (this was confirmed by quite senior officers). Were they real, an invention, or an illusion produced by the stress of

battle? They were certainly a useful propaganda tool to demonstrate that God was really on their side!

Any belief in angels, whether they be on one side or another, must be based on faith and those of great faith are more likely to have such experiences.

Among the angelic encounters of the great religious figures two in particular stand out: those of St. Francis of Assisi and St. Teresa of Avila.

On retreat at La Verna in 1224, St. Francis prayed that he might experience the physical agony of the crucified Christ and was rewarded with an angelic vision in which he received the stigmata, purplish marks on palms, feet and side which match the Five Wounds of Jesus made by the nails of the

LEFT
The Temptation of St. Thomas Aquinas *by Diego Rodriguez de Silva y Velasquez (1599-1660). In his youth the family of this learned 13th-century theologian was said to have been concerned by his excessive devotion to study and brought an attractive young woman into his room. Taking a burning brand from the fire, he drew a cross upon the wall and drove her out. Here, as the rejected girl departs, one angel helps the future saint recover from the shock while another brings him a belt of chastity which was to render him immune from any future temptation of a sexual nature.* Orihuela Cathedral Museum.

ABOVE
The Stigmata of St. Francis *by Bonaventura Berlinghieri (1228-1278). The founder of the Franciscan Order is well known for preaching to the birds and his belief in the kinship of man with nature. Here he receives the marks on hands, feet and side, which correspond to the wounds of Christ, from an angel who appears in the form of Christ on the Cross.* Galleria degli Uffizi, Florence.

crucifixion and the spear of the Roman guard. The stigmata was transmitted to him by a six-winged seraph in the form of the crucified Christ. He also had a vision in which he heard angelic music and on his death was said to have been carried up to heaven to become Rhamiel, the Angel of Mercy.

St. Bonaventure, his successor, who wrote a *Life of St. Francis*, considered that he had achieved the equivalent of martyrdom through the fire of his love which had consumed his soul causing him to become even greater than an angel.

This consuming love was also a feature of St.Teresa's life 300 years later. She often had visions of angels but only rarely saw what she took to be cherubim.

On one remarkable occasion, a short but very beautiful cherubim appeared all afire, especially his face, holding a long golden spear with a flaming iron tip. She described how

... he seemed to pierce my heart several times to my very entrails, and when he drew it out I thought he was drawing them out with it. I was left completely afire and with a great love of God. The sharpness of the pain made me moan several times and so intense was the sweetness that this intense pain brought me that one would never wish to lose it, nor will one's soul be content with anything less than God.'

Communion with angels seems to be a corollary of such religious ecstasy, whether as an actual physical manifestation or as a dream-like vision.

Angels of Judgement

Both Christians and Moslems look forward to a final Day of Judgement when the trumpet calls of the Archangel Gabriel will rouse the dead and all creation will be brought before God to be raised to paradise or cast into eternal damnation. Mankind, jinni and angels will all be judged. The angels of heaven will be busily employed in organizing and supervising and, though perhaps the angelic administrators and marshalls will themselves be judged after their work is done, it would be logical that God will already have selected the most worthy so that they should have no difficulty in judging their fellows. The task will be enormous, for according to Islamic accounting, mankind makes up only one per cent of creation, jinni being nine times as numerous with angels forming the other 90 per cent: they total 100 times the number of human lives to have been lived since creation.

The best known apocalypse, or revelation, of what the end of the world will be like is in the canonical *Book of Revelation of St. John the Divine*, claimed to be a record of a vision received by the saint when a prisoner on the island of Patmos. It was once believed that he was synonymous with with writer of St. John's Gospel and the beloved disciple John, but scholars now question this. He was thought to have lived to a great age but was told by Christ when his end was near and dug his own grave ready and lay in it. There was then a blinding light and when his followers regained their vision his body had disappeared: it was believed to have been taken straight up to heaven and, like Elijah, become an angel.

His Revelation – which he is instructed to send to the angels of the Christian communities in various countries (presumably in this case angel means human beings responsible for passing on the divine message), tells of destruction wrought upon the earth, of war in heaven, of the battle at Armageddon, of judgement and the

The Good Being Led to Heaven (*detail*) by *Rogier van der Weyden (1399-1464)*. Hôtel Dieu, Beaune.

The Pillared Angel, *woodcut by Albrecht Dürer (1471-1528). The artist here illustrates what the* Book of Revelation *describes as 'another mighty angel came down from heaven, clothed with a cloud, and a rainbow was upon his head, and his face was as it were the sun, and his feet were as pillars of fire.'*

creation of a new heaven and a new earth. At every stage angels are at work, spreading plague, famine, earthquake, war; fighting the armies of the devil, marking the devout with a seal on their foreheads, chaining up the devil and then releasing him after a thousand years, sounding trumpets, assisting in the giving of judgement and attending the coming of the new Jerusalem.

The final judgement comes as John witnessed the fact that:
'the dead, the small and the great, stand before God; and the books were opened: and another book was opened, which is the book of life: and the dead were judged out of those things which were written in the books, according to their works.'

These books must contain records made either during life or at an interrogation after death. Christian tradition has one or more recording angels, given various names, who, when a person dies, passes on the information about their life to Azrael, Angel of Death, or to Michael who balances each soul's virtue against its evil. In Islam, the roles are divided between four angels. A pair of blue-eyed, black angels are responsible for questioning the deceased, Mungkar (or Monker) and Nekir, while Raquib writes down the good deeds done in life and Atib records the bad.

Paradise of the Symbolic Fountain *by Dieric Bouts (c. 1448-1475). An archangel leads the saved into paradise.* Musée des Beaux-Arts, Lille.

The Last Judgement by Hieronymous Bosch (1450-1516).
Christ in Majesty sits on the judgement seat, flanked by saints, His mother at His right hand, while angels left and right sound their trumpets.

Below, angels vanquish demons, while in the background others help the risen dead from their graves, leading the virtuous towards the paradise garden on the left and off to hell on the right.

PHOTOGRAPHIC ACKNOWLEDGEMENTS

Jacket front cover: Angel by Thayer: The Bridgeman Art Library, London.
Jacket back cover: Jacob's Dream by Cardi da Cigoli The Bridgeman Art Library, London.

By permission of The Bridgeman Art Library, London: Detailed acknowledgements below: 1, 2-3, 6, 8-9, 10-11, 12, 17, 19, 20, 21, 22, 23, 26 top and bottom, 27, 28, 28 right, 29 left, 30, 31 right, 32 left and right, 33, 34, 35, 36,37 right, 38-39, 40 right, 41 top and bottom, 42, 43 top, 44 left, 44 right, 45, 46, 47, 48 top and bottom, 50, 51, 52, 52-53 54, 55, 56-57, 58, 59, 60, 61, 62, 63, 64 left and right, 65, 66 bottom, 67, top and bottom, 68 top and bottom, 69, 70 top and bottom, 71 left and right, 72 left and right, 73 left and right, 74 right, 75 left and right, 76 left, 77.

Angel by Thayer, Abbott Handerson; National Museum of American Art, Smithsonian Inst./Bridgeman Art Library London: Jacob's Dream by Cardi da Cigoli, Ludovico; Musée des Beaux-Arts, Nancy/Bridgeman Art Library London/Giraudon: The Annunciation by Crivelli, Carlo; National Gallery, London/Bridgeman Art Library, London: St. Margaret of Antioch by Natoire, Charles Joseph; Phillips, The International Fine Art Auctioneers/Bridgeman Art Library: Annunciation by Botticelli, Sandro; Galleria degli Uffizi, Florence/Bridgeman Art Library, London: Baptism of Christ by Albani, Francesco; Phillips, The International Fine Art Auctioneers/Bridgeman Art Library London: The Good being led to Heaven (detail) by Weyden, Rogier van der; Hotel Dieu, Beaune/Bridgeman Art Library London: Abraham's Sacrifice by Rembrandt, Hermensz van Rijn; Hermitage, St. Petersburg/Bridgeman Art Library London: Detail of Heaven from the Last Judgement by Angelico, Fra (Guido di Pietro); Museo di San Marco dell'Angelico, Florence/Bridgeman Art Library London: The Annunciation by Angelico, Fra (Guido di Pietro) Museo Diocesano, Cortona/Bridgeman Art Library London: The Annunciation from the Isenheim Altarpiece by Grunewald, Mattias; Unterlinden Museum, Colmar, France/Bridgeman Art Library London: Lot and His Daughters Leaving Sodom by Caullery, Louis de; Rafael Valls Gallery, London/Bridgeman Art Library London: The Immaculate Conception by Antolinez Jose; Prado, Madrid/Bridgeman Art Library London: Lansdowne The Maries at the sepulchre, England Shaftesbury Psalter; British Library, London/Bridgeman Art Library: The Three Maries at Christ's Grave by Eyck, H van & Eyckm J. van; Museum Boymans van Beuningen, Rotterdam/Bridgeman Art Library London: Flight into Egypt by Meloni, Marco; Roy Miles Gallery, 29 Bruton Street, London W1/Bridgeman Art Library: Concert of Angels from the Isenheim Altarpiece by Grunewald, Mattias; Unterlinden Museum, Colmar, France/Bridgeman Art Library London: Abraham and the Three Angels by Tiepolo, Giovanni Domenico; Galleria dell' Accademia, Venice/Bridgeman Art Library London: The Story of Adam and Eve, detail from 'Cas des Nobles Hommes et Femmes' by Boccaccio, translated by Laurent de Premierfait, French, 1465 Works of Giovanni Boccaccio; Musée Conde, Chantilly/Bridgeman Art Library London: Paradise of the Symbolic Fountain by Bouts, Dirck; Musée des Beaux-Arts, Lille/Bridgeman Art Library London: Temptation of St. Thomas Aquinas (& 2 details) by Velasques, Diego Rodriguez de Silva y; Orihuela Cathedral Museum/Bridgeman Art Library London: The Lamentation of Christ by Daret, Jean; Musée de Beaux-Arts, Marseilles/Bridgeman Art Library London: The Annunciation by Tintoretto, Jacopo; Scuola Grande di San Rocco, Venice/Bridgeman Art Library London: Madonna under a Baldachin by Botticelli, Sandro; Biblioteca Ambrosiana, Milan/Bridgeman Art Library, London: The Ramparts of God's House by Strudwich, Johm Melhuish; Christie's, London/Bridgeman Art Library London: St. Michael and the Dragon by Bermejo, (Bartolome de Cardenas) Werner Collection, Luton Hoo, Bedfordshire/Bridgeman Art Library London: Left panel from the Ghen Altarpiece, by Eyck, Jan van; St. Bavo Cathedral, Ghent/Bridgeman Art Library London/Giraudon: Archangel Gabriel by Arpo, Guarieto de; Museo Bottacin e Museo Civico, Padua/Bridgeman Art Library London: The Angel of Death; Osterreichische Nationalbibliothek, Vienna/Bridgeman Art Library London: The Angel of Death by Morgan, Evelyn de; The De Morgan Foundation, London/Bridgeman Art Library, London: St. Michael fighting the Devil by Jacob Epstein; Coventry Cathedral, Warks/Bridgeman Art Library

London: Sistine Chapel Ceiling, Creation of Adam by Michelangelo, Buonarroti; Vatican Museums & Galleries, Rome/Bridgeman Art Library: Jacob's Ladder by Blake, William; British Library, London/Bridgeman Art Library London: Balaam's Ass by Bol, Hans; Johnny van Haeften Gallery, London/Bridgeman Art Library London: St. Joseph and the Angel by Tour, Georges de la; Wrightsman Collection, New York/Bridgeman Art Library London: The morning of the resurrection (oil on panel) by Burne-Jones, Sir Edward; Christie's, London/Bridgeman Art Library London: Coventry Cathedral; The Chapel of Christ in Gethsemane, Archangel with Three Sleeping Diciples; Relief mural in cement fondu by Stefan Sykes; screened off by black steel crown of thorns designed by Basil Spence (photo credit) The Bridgeman Art Library London: The Dream of St. Jerome by Pietro, Nicoli di; Louvre, Paris/Bridgeman Art Library London: St. Sebastian by Sodoma, Giovanni Antonio Bazzi; Palazzi Pitti, Florence/Bridgeman Art Library: God presenting Eve to Adam by Boucicaut Master & Workshop Bibliotheque Nationale, Paris/Bridgeman Art Library: Ascent of the Prophet Muhammad to Heaven, by Aqa Mirak; British Library, London/Bridgeman Art Library London: Ecce Ancilla Domini by Rossetti, Dante Gabriel; Tate Gallery, London/Bridgeman Art Library London: Mystic Nativity by Botticelli, Sandro; National Gallery, London/Bridgeman Art Libray London: The Agony in the Garden by Goya y Lucientes, Francisco Jose de; Christie's London/Bridgeman Art Library London: The Mourning by Hicks, George Elgar; Forbes Magazine Collection, New York/Bridgeman Art Library London: St. Luke by Mabuse, Peter; Kunsthistorisches Museum, Vienna/Bridgeman Art Library London: Angesl, from the Lamentation, by Giotto, Ambrogio Bondone; Scrovegni (Arena) Chapel, Padua/Bridgeman Art Library London: The Virgin enthroned, wiht angels and saints by Perugino, Pietro; Galleria dell'Accademia, Florence/Bridgeman Art Library London: The Lamentation of Christ by Giotto, Ambrogio Bondone; Scrovegni (Arena) Chapel Padua/Bridgeman Art Library, London: The Virgin in a Rose Arbour by Lochner, Stephan; Wallraf-Richartz Museum, cologne/Bridgeman Art Library London: Satan and the Rebel Angels, by Blake, William; Victoria & Albert Musem, London/Bridgeman Art Library London: Tapestry, part of a curtain, wool and linen; Victorial & Albert Museum, London/Bridgeman Art Library London: Hebrew biblical text, showing the Ark of the Covenant; British Library, London/Bridgeman Art Library London: St. Michael by Zenale, Bernadion; Galleria degli Uffizi, Florence/Bridgeman Art Library London: The Fall of the Rebel Angels by Ricci, Sebastiano; Dulwich Picture Gallery, London/Bridgeman Art Library London: Hagar in the desert by Batoni, Pompeo Girolamo; Galleria Nazionale d'Arte Antica, Rome/Bridgeman Art Library London: Fight between Jacob and the Angel by Delacroix, Eugene; St. Sulpice, Paris/Bridgeman Art Library London/Giraudon: The Ascension of Elijah, Icon by Pskov School; State Russian Museum, St. Petersburg/Bridgeman Art Library London: St. Michael, by Pol de Limbourg, Tres Riches Heures du Duc de Berry; Musée Conde, Chantilly/Bridgeman Art Library/Giraudon: Kings; God's Vengence on Assyria (printed book) Nuremberg Bible; Victoria & Albert Museum/Bridgeman Art Library London: Elijah Visited by an Angel by Moretto, Alessandro Bonvicino San Giovanni Evangelista, Bresicia/Bridgeman Art Library London: Fall of the rebel angels; Tres Riches Heures du Duc de Berry; Musée Conde, Chantilly/Bridgeman Art Library London: The Liberation of St. Peter by Raphael, Sanzio of Urbino; Vatican Museums & Galleries, Rome/Bridgeman Art Library London: Tobias and the Archangel Raphael (panel) by Titian, Tiziano Vecelli; Galleria dell'Accademia, Venice, Bridgeman Art Library London: Tobias and the Archangel Raphael by Cazin, Jean-Charles; Musée des Beaux-Arts, Lille/Bridgeman Art Library London: Israelites passing through the Wilderness by West, William; City of Bristol Museum and Art Gallery/Bridgeman Art Library London: Agony in the Garden by Mantegna, Andrea; National Gallery, London/Bridgeman Art Library London: The Assumption by Veronese, Paolo Callari; Galleria dell'Accademia, Venice/Bridgeman Art Library London: The Stigmata of St. Francis by Berlinghieri, Bonaventura; Galleria degli Uffizi, Florence/ Bridgeman Art Library London: Vision of St. Theresa by Amigoni, Jacopo; Phillips, The International Fine Art Auctioneers/Bridgeman Art Library London: St. Joseph and the Christ child by El Greco, Domenicos Theolocopoulos; Toledo Caehdral Castile; Bridgeman Art Library London: Adoration of the Magi, detail from an

altarpiece by Mantegna, Andrea; Galleria degli Uffizi, Florence/Bridgeman Art Library London: Christ Child Adored by Angels, Central panel of a Goes, Hugo van der the Portinari Altarpiece; Galleria degli Uffizi, Florence/Bridgeman Art Library London: Annunciation to the Shepherds by Berchem, Nicolaes; City of Briston Museum and Art Gallery/Bridgeman Art Library London: The Annunciation (panel) by Vinci, Leonardo da; Galleria degli Uffizi, Florence/Bridgeman Art Library London: St. Vincent Ferrer Altarpiece by Bellini, Giovanni San Giovanni e Paolo, Venice/Bridgeman Art Library London: Silos Apocalypse; Daniel's vision by Mozarabic Apocalypse, 1109 of the Four Beasts and God enthroned; British Library/Bridgeman Art Library London: Gathering of the Manna, from the Altarpiece of the by Bouts, Dirck Last Supper; St. Peter's, Leuven/Bridgeman Art Library London: The Annunciation by Angelico, Fra (Guido di Pietro) Museo di San Marco dell'Angelico, Florence/Bridgeman Art Library London: Angel musician by Forli, Melozzo da; Vatican Museums & Galleries, Rome/Bridgeman Art Library London: La Destin by Eileen Gray; Private Collection/Bridgeman Art Library London.

The British Library: 49.

E.T. Archive 16, 18, 31 left, 37 left, 77 right.

H. Loxton: 24.

The National Gallery, London: 14-15.